Tradition » Passion » Perfection

Simon Crompton is the founder of Permanent Style,
the most popular blog on men's classic style in the UK.
The site is read worldwide and in 2008 was named one
of the top 10 style blogs by *The New York Times*. Simon
is also Editor-in-Chief of Gentleman's Corner, a website
celebrating men's dress, and writes regularly for
The Financial Times and *The Rake* magazine.

Conceived and produced by
Elwin Street Productions
144 Liverpool Road
London N1 1LA
www.elwinstreet.com

Hardie Grant Books (Australia)
658 Church St
Richmond
Victoria 3121
www.hardiegrant.com.au

Hardie Grant Books (UK)
34-35 Southhampton Street
London WC2E 7HF
www.hardiegrant.co.uk

ISBN: 978-174270169-1

Illustrations: Tonwen Jones

Picture credits:
Getty: p. 47; Guy Hills: pp. 25, 77, 111;
Christopher Simon Sykes: p. 71.

Printed in China

TAILORING

Simon Crompton

hardie grant books

MELBOURNE · LONDON

Contents

Why be a snob about tailoring?

A well-fitting suit is incredibly flattering, but there is a lot of ignorance among men about how to get one. Ready to wear is underused; made to measure is ignored; bespoke is misunderstood. It's not hard to become educated, and a snob, about tailoring. All you need is a little passion.

A well-made suit can change the way you feel about yourself – a suit tailored to your unique physique means the fit will be perfect and comfortable. A bespoke suit flatters all shapes. It makes you look thinner, fitter, stronger: perhaps all of the above. Some tailors will give the jacket a sharply cut waist yet retain a little 'drape' in the chest, diminishing the former and exaggerating the latter. The V of the chest will accentuate your shoulders and suggest athletic shape, and can increase your confidence, just by looking in the mirror.

Bespoke also allows you to design your own clothes. It means you can put your personality into what you wear. Whether that's the subtle touches of brown horn buttons and turn-ups, or the loud flair of pink pinstripes and lime-green lining, it is personal and unique to you. There are a lot of options out there on the high street, but each is more a question of copying someone else's ideas than coming up with your own. And there's always the risk that you will see 'yourself' coming towards you down the street, wearing exactly the same suit.

Not everyone uses bespoke just for suits. My tailor has made cycling jerseys, cropped jackets and capes, to name a few. It's limited only by what you can imagine. Of course suits make up the majority of bespoke clothing and most of this book will be concerned with them. But many of the principles, from cloth selection to tips on the fitting process, apply equally well to other types of dress.

A great suit is always worth investing in, whether bespoke or not. For the most important times of your life, it gives you and your attire a sense of occasion. It is smart, sleek and serious. If worn every day in the office, it will become a stamp of quiet authority that stays with you through the week, and with others. It can affect how they see you.

For men, dressing well is undeniably a source of unexplored pleasure; clothes are the last area where modern man feels he cannot be seen to be making an effort. So he doesn't.

That's his first mistake. The effort should never be seen, whether you're into clothes or not. The best style is casual, easy, nonchalant. It's just something you threw on in the morning. And such is the quality of your wardrobe and your accumulated taste that it may actually be what you just threw on that morning.

Tailoring can be scary. It's not easy to know how to describe what you want or whether you're getting value for money. That anxiety is dispelled by knowledge, which is what this book endeavours to provide. Whether you're bespeaking a whole new suit or just having some jeans altered, the facts you need are here.

Tailors are wonderfully old-fashioned. It means they create suits that last as well as those of a century ago; and they will fit better than anything else, such is the focus on fit. However, it does make their language a little antiquated. I have even heard one use 'bespoke' in its original meaning, as a piece of cloth that was "bespoken" for.

One thing that all Savile Row tailors, and many others besides, insist on is calling the top half of a suit, the 'coat'. Historically, this is correct. That's why we have overcoats – they were worn over the coat. Today, however, an overcoat has been shortened to a coat and a coat is universally referred to as a jacket.

Because of this universal recognition, I will refer to this item of clothing as a jacket throughout this book. Tailors will hate me for it. But this book is for you, not them.

» Fundamentals

Ready to wear, made to measure and bespoke

The distinction between the three main categories of suit – ready to wear, made to measure and bespoke – is really one of fit. While a bespoke suit will normally be better made than one that is ready to wear (RTW), this is not always or necessarily the case.

Ready to wear

Italian houses like Kiton and Brioni make RTW suits that are superior in quality to some off-Savile Row tailors. So as much as people include hand construction in the definition of bespoke, it's best to think of it as a question of fit. And it's perfectly possible to achieve a good fit with RTW – the key is to understand the sizing, shop around and have the suit altered if needed.

Made to measure

Made to measure (MTM) is simply an extension of this logic. It takes standard sizes and adjusts them in more ways than you would ever bother to do with an alterations tailor. The suit will likely be made by a machine in the same factory as RTW. The job will be done by a smaller, specialised machine that is able to do very short runs or individual jobs. It isn't quite bespoke, but it will fit you very well. The advice on both being measured for a MTM suit and selecting its design are the same as for bespoke, and almost equally as important.

Bespoke

Bespoke, however, is different in one key way – the pattern is yours and yours alone. Once the tailor has taken all your measurements (around 12–15 normally – more than MTM), he will translate those onto a unique pattern. He will take a piece of brown paper and mark out a chest piece – one half of the front of your prospective suit – using your measurements, figuration and 'rock of eye'.

Figuration is everything about the shape of a man that is not expressed in simple measuring, like the balance of your shoulder blades, hips or stoop. A tailor's rock of eye is his ability to reproduce a mental picture of how the customer stood and presented himself, in order to further inform the pattern to be created.

The paper pattern is what defines bespoke; it is more personal and precise than any other form of suit-fitting. It is used to cut sections of cloth that will be 'basted' together (sewn using loose, long stitches that can easily be pulled out) and hung on the customer at his first fitting. At this basted fitting the tailor will chalk on many little changes and alterations, 'rip it down' (pull out the basting stitches) and re-cut the cloth to this new shape. The paper pattern will also be adjusted accordingly, by either taping on or cutting off slivers of paper.

These levels of attention to fit are what distinguish RTW, MTM and bespoke: mass production, individual production or painstaking paper.

International styles

The story of the suit is largely an English story, driven by the role of empire, commerce and cultural colonialism. And in England, the main players were often princes of Wales – three usually come up in relation to style: King Edward VII, the Duke of Windsor (briefly Edward VIII) and Prince Charles. Modern men often wonder why two British princes made such an impact on the world of menswear. One reason is certainly that royalty was revered and looked up to. Once the prince had worn it, you had confidence wearing an otherwise daring piece of clothing. The stamp of approval meant much.

But an equal reason was that people saw pictures of royalty far more than anyone else. With little advertising, magazines or alternative celebrities, royal members were the only pin-ups available. If one of them had genuine character and style, their lasting fame was inevitable.

The influence of the Italians

Possibly the biggest effect on how sartorialism is viewed today comes from the influence of the Italians in the latter half of the twentieth century. Everyone thinks the Italians look good, they are a daily inspiration the world over.

Where the English gentleman might generally experiment with relatively hidden items of clothing – red socks, brightly striped shirts, amusingly patterned braces – by his standard attire of dark suit, black shoes and club tie, the Italian keeps these

›› Take pleasure in dressing well

It's a real shame that society has come to a point where people who wish to dress with style feel embarrassed to do so, that they feel they can't sport a suit and tie and pocket handkerchief because of how it will be perceived. So few people today realise that one can derive pleasure from the act of dressing each morning. It can be a most enjoyable quiet, slightly introspective pause in your otherwise hectic schedule.

Dressing well is not simple, but the older you get the easier it becomes. Our shirtmaker has been around Savile Row and Jermyn Street for 35 years now and he has a terrific eye for clothes. And it's always something with a little colour, not just a plain dark tie, a pale shirt and a dark suit.

There should be no shame in picking up on what others do. If somebody comes into my shop wearing something really fantastic I write it all down. There's nothing wrong with learning a lesson from our elders and betters.

consistent. He wears a blue shirt and navy tie a lot of the time, allowing him to wear more flannel, linen and coloured shoes.

I coined the phrase 'Italian background' to describe this blue shirt/blue tie combination, as it is an ideal, neutral background for experimentation elsewhere. In the summer in Milan you will see far more men wear tan linen suits than ever in London (weather aside), but wearing an Italian background underneath that linen suit somehow makes the whole ensemble look conservative.

Royal influences

Edward VII of the UK helped create the dinner jacket as an alternative for evening wear. He brought back the black Homburg hat from Germany, favoured turn-ups on trousers and allegedly left the bottom button of his waistcoat undone after a large repast, which created a trend overnight.

His grandson, the Duke of Windsor, also had a number of stylistic innovations: a double-breasted suit during the day, which removed the necessity of a waistcoat; belts with trousers, rather than braces; zip flies rather than buttons; and, most famous of all, a more relaxed tailoring pioneered by Frederick Scholte – now known as the London cut, or the drape.

Sprezzatura

The Italian style icons tend to be those that follow this look and then add small innovations of their own. But these are innovations more deliberately casual than the English. They require palpable *sprezzatura*.

Unlike most other countries, the Italians have one man that stands head and shoulders above all other style icons. His name was Gianni Agnelli. Long the CEO of Fiat and a man of politics as well as business, Agnelli was admired for his ability to meld strict conservatism with personal quirks that everyone seemed to notice apart from him. Agnelli always wore his watches on the outside of his shirt cuff. He claimed this was because the band of the watch irritated his skin. Perhaps. But there had to be other types of strap that would not irritate. No, he wore his watch over his cuff because he tried it once (for whatever reason) and liked the style. So he did it again and again until it felt natural. Until it was, and everyone would see that it was.

He wore a lot of flannel. He wore a lot of woollen ties. He famously patronised the Tod's winter boot when one was sent to him by an enterprising Diego Della Valle. But in every photo of the great man he looks serious, business-like, conservative, and his quirks do not undermine that; he is not wearing braces with little pheasants on them, as Englishmen have been known to do.

The classic suit styles

Most men have a pretty good idea what a suit looks like. In their mind, it will be single breasted, have two or three buttons and notch lapels, and the trousers will sit on the hips and probably not have pleats or turn-ups. But many will probably not be able to describe the suit in these terms. So when presented with the question 'what style of suit would you like?' by their tailor, they will struggle.

Before you can answer that question with confidence, you have to be able to understand some key points of reference, and the advantages of a double-breasted suit, a cuffed suit or a pleated suit, so that you can

Three-button single breasted jacket with notched lapels

Three-button jacket with natural roll and notched lapels make your choices accordingly, and know exactly what you want before you attempt to describe it.

Let's start with a single-breasted jacket. The first thing to decide on is the number of buttons, which is more complicated than it sounds and drives many other decisions. Then, consider ways to flatter your shape – everyone has something they would rather accentuate or hide.

The importance of buttons

Fashions exist even within classic menswear, and over the decades the dominant number of buttons has varied between one, two, three and even four. But the reign of the first and last of those was quite brief – generally the most common style has either been a two- or three-button front.

Two-button single-breasted jacket with notched lapels

Double-breasted jacket with peak lapels

Short lapels

Ten years ago, three buttons were definitely the most fashionable. But there's true three-buttons and three-buttons that roll. A true three-button jacket will have lapels that end, abruptly, just above the top of those buttons. When only the waist button (the middle one of the three) is fastened, this short lapel will create a sharp, rather awkward angle at the top of the jacket's front. It has been designed to button the top two, and looks odd if they are not both fastened.

Natural roll

The style with short lapels is one extreme. Most other jackets will have some amount of roll to them, so that when the top button is not fastened, the lapel rolls back and lengthens, ending somewhere above the waist button. The ease of the roll will depend on the canvassing of the chest and the stitching behind the lapel. A more heavily canvassed jacket, for example, cannot roll as easily, because of its heavier and firmer lining, while a more structured jacket will also often have stitching behind the lapel that holds it in a particular shape. Lightweight jackets sometimes have this stitching to avoid losing the shape altogether.

High fastening

High fastenings look good on fewer people, as they shorten the plunge of the lapel and reduce that uniquely elongating, strengthening effect of a good jacket. Four button and true three-button jackets have been most popular in the past when driven by specific fashions, such as the Mods or the Teddy

Boys in England. And indeed both of those inherited parts of their look from earlier gentleman's attire where as little shirting was on display as possible – leading to the necessity of a high-fastening jacket or an ever-present waistcoat.

So you might want to eschew a true three-button jacket in favour of the more natural 'three-rolls-to-two' style, which is both more flexible and flattering than its peers. This will be less of a problem in the US, which has always favoured more relaxed and less structured jackets. The higher fastening, being

Peak lapels

The peak lapel comes from the morning coat that was the standard dress for Victorians in England and formal attire for decades afterwards.

A dinner jacket should have peaked lapels because it is a descendant of this coat, the tails being lopped off to make the look more casual. Equally, the overlooked 'stroller' jacket style also has peaked lapels. This is a black jacket without tails and without the silk facings of a dinner jacket, but often worn formally with grey trousers and made from a luxurious cloth such as cashmere.

There is nothing necessarily wrong with peaked lapels on a single-breasted suit jacket. Just bear in mind that they are more formal than notch lapels, and should be treated as such.

tighter, buttoned up and necessarily of a narrower cut, has historically found more favour in fashion in France and Italy. If you're going with three buttons, make sure they roll.

Fewer buttons

So a higher fastening is less flattering and, generally, less stylish, and fewer buttons both lengthens a man and emphasises his shoulders. You could be forgiven for thinking that the choice of one button or two takes this argument a step further, but in fact the lapel length will likely be the same. With both styles, the waist button is the top (or only) fastening – the two-button style merely adds another, lower button.

What's more, most two-button jackets are designed for the bottom button not to be done up. You can fasten it, unlike the bottom buttons of some waistcoats, but the cut is far more elegant without. (Some styles have two buttons that sit above and below the waist, and are designed to both be fastened. JFK was famously pictured in a couple. But these are rare, often fashion ephemera, and blunter than a traditional shape. After all, why turn that single-point fulcrum into a static bar? It denies movement to a suit.)

The second button

So, you may well ask, what is the point of a second button? It seems redundant. Many commentators have shared this view, alleging that one button looks more stylish and three more practical, while a two-button jacket is just dull. There are three principal reasons for adding the second button.

The first is practical – a little wind can turn your jacket fronts inside out, flapping them around and forcing you to repress them with your hands. That's not exactly elegant and ruins whatever silhouette was intended by the cut. The second is a matter of style: one button is sharp, singular, not to say rakish. Dashing to some, louche to others, it is certainly a statement. No matter the jacket's heritage – coming from the morning coat and riding wear – nor its superb modern manifestation (thanks to Huntsman and latterly Richard Anderson), this is a style. And some men don't want a style – they want normal, they want unobtrusive, they want stolid. They do not want anything that could suggest a rake. For them, the two-button jacket is flattering and practical.

High-waisted trousers

Finally, and perhaps least importantly for today's man and style trends, a one-button jacket should really have high-waisted trousers. Back when all men wore braces, their trousers all started around their belly button, so the waist of the trousers and of the jacket were both on their natural waist. This meant that when they put their hands in their pockets, pulling apart the jacket, no shirting was on display. While this isn't necessarily recommended for every modern man, a triangle of puffy shirt is hardly flattering and negates the upward-sweeping triangle of the lapels.

So as a one-button jacket means more of a cutaway front, there is more potential for displaying your waist in this way. Trousers on the natural waist are not required, but the argument for them strengthens.

And few men wear trousers of that height today. One versus two-button is a matter of personality, but consider the arguments on both sides.

Re-consider a double breast

Some men prefer a double-breasted jacket because it can add width to slimmer shoulders. However, this does not have to be the effect of a double-breasted. Much of the impact is a result of design that can be personalised – the position of the buttons, and their number, makes a big difference, for example.

A double-breasted front creates immediate width because the foreparts cross over each other rather than joining together. So the lapel runs at an angle across the body, and is usually peaked – accentuating the diagonal. The buttons also create width because they run horizontally as well as vertically.

Reducing the width

That squareness and width can easily be mitigated. First, the line of the lapel can be altered radically by the position of the waist button and how far the two foreparts cross over. Imagine a standard double-breasted jacket. Now move the waist button (normally in the middle row of a six-button front, or the top row of a four-button) slowly down. Notice how the slope of the lapel lessens – as the top is fixed at the collar, but the bottom is moving downwards, the line has to straighten up. Now gradually reduce the overlap, so the waist button moves towards the centre of the jacket. Again this straightens the lapel (though also shortening it slightly). Don't push this too far, but you'll be amazed what a difference just an inch or even a half-inch makes.

So when you are having a bespoke suit made, consider the position of the waist button and the extent of the overlap. You can even go for a 6x2 or 4x2 design, where only the bottom buttons look like they fasten. The first of these is not to everyone's taste and can look too bulky, but the second is definitely an option with a four-button front. They're also hard to find in the shops today, so it highlights a bespoke design.

Reducing the number of buttons helps too. Four buttons will look less bulky than six, or you can just have two. This last option looks more fashionable than traditional, but then you can always add more buttons later – another advantage of bespoke.

Also, a large man can wear double-breasted much more easily if he reduces its bulk in every other way, through lack of clutter, texture and excess cloth. Large men shouldn't be scared of a double-breasted suit, and slim men should positively embrace it.

In the details

Lined and unlined jackets,
and everything in between

» Suit lining

Most suits will be fully lined, but they can also be
half lined (also known as 'buggy lining'), quarter
lined or even unlined. Mostly this is done to save
weight and increase breathability in summer suits.

A half lining stops at the side seams, leaving the
back exposed save for one or two sections across the
neck to make it sit cleanly. A quarter lining stops half
way to the side seam. An unlined jacket has no
lining, though similar material will be used to tape
the seams everywhere inside.

Although jackets with less than full lining require
less material, they usually take longer to construct
and so can be more expensive. Within the cloak of a
lining a tailor can get away with a multitude of sins
with his seams and loose threads. Without that cloak
every stitch must be finished perfectly.

Choosing a shape

The subtleties of a suit's design can make a disproportionate difference to how it flatters your figure. Tall or short, broad or narrow, even average build, there are things you should consider whether buying a suit or commissioning bespoke.

Accentuating a shorter stature

To accentuate your height, you need to avoid any excess cloth as this will add to your bulk and hence your short stature, so go with a close, not to say a narrow, fit. On the jacket you should go for one button, or two at a maximum. The more buttons there are, the more horizontal points break up the front of the jacket, and, probably more importantly, the shorter the lapels have to be.

The sweep of a suit's lapel from neck to waist is the strongest line in the suit and potentially its most flattering. So keep that line as long as possible if you want to appear taller. The difference between one and two buttons is small, as the waist button will not move much with the addition of a button below it.

The jacket's waist should be quite tight, or 'suppressed', in line with the theme of keeping cloth to a minimum. The waist of the trousers, meanwhile, should be high and at a man's natural waist (around the belly button, if not higher). This may feel unnatural to some, but it does make the legs appear longer and produce cleaner lines in the pleats as they drop over the hip bone. If you go for a lower rise, make sure you have slim legs and sharp creases on the trousers.

The jacket should be relatively short in order to, again, lengthen the legs. Nothing is worse for a short man than a jacket that swamps him, whether on the arms, waist or hips. High vents will add to the impression of height; though if you can resist the urge to put your hands in your pockets, a ventless jacket is even better.

Anything that removes bulk from the look of the suit is also beneficial. So avoid ticket pockets, large pocket flaps, patch pockets, pocket handkerchiefs and cuffs on either the sleeves or trousers. They all interrupt the long, clean lines we're aiming for. If the notch in the lapel can be a little higher, that will also help.

Think of bulk when choosing the cloth as well: darker, finer wools will create a sharp silhouette. You should avoid pale tones, bright colours and large patterns (particularly checks), although a fine pinstripe can elongate your shape. As to the rest of the outfit, dark shoes and a simple tie will accentuate the look, and avoid the contrast of sports jackets or odd waistcoats.

Interrupt a tall man

Now reverse all that for a tall man. Interrupt the look at every possible opportunity: ticket pockets, patch pockets, broad checks and odd jackets. Wear a belt, have trouser cuffs and buy some brogues – the more texture the better. Throw the eye sideways with a pocket handkerchief; eschew a smooth silk tie; wear a waistcoat; wear a watch; have your sleeves a touch shorter so there is always a half-inch of shirt cuff – anything to break up the lines.

Tall men and narrow men have the same tools at their disposal. The thin should ape the tactics of the tall man, the large man those of the short. If you are tall and stout, or thin and short, consider your priorities and apply accordingly. Men tend to want to avoid the latter of those two pairs most.

The loose style of Fred Astaire

Fred Astaire was known for introducing a relaxed, easy-going feel to his clothes. He ensured that the armholes on his jackets were always cut high and tight, to give his arms greater freedom to move without dragging the rest of the jacket with him. He famously jumped around the fitting room at his tailor Anderson & Sheppard, stopping suddenly to glance in the mirror and check his collar was still tight to the back of his neck.

Astaire's clothes were not cut loose to help him dance. Rather, he wore larger clothes because he wished to hide his slim physique. Whenever one sees images of him, it is notable that his neck, wrists or ankles are always very thin compared to the volume of his clothes. It is a credit to Astaire's tailors that this never looked out of place or drew attention.

How to pick colour

For business or generally formal suits, colour is pretty simple, but there are a few ways to make sure you're getting it just right.

A standard blue

The standard colours are blue and grey, and for good reason: no other colours can both look smart and flatter a man's skin tone at the same time. Black is too harsh; brown isn't smart enough; tan is downright casual.

The colour needs to be dark to be businesslike, but that doesn't mean it should be almost black. Navy is the classic blue for business suits – while a dark shade, it is easily distinguishable from black, and is definitely blue. Too many men buy suits that are too dark (closer to midnight blue, a tone often used for eveningwear and which looks black until closely inspected), and make them look pale and pasty. Real blues and greys are much kinder.

A navy or mid-blue is also far more interesting in terms of colour combinations. Midnight blue looks very smart with a white shirt and black shoes, but that's about it. Navy, on the other hand, also looks good with those accessories, but brings out chocolate-brown shoes as well. And a blue shirt provides a great background for experimentation with colour in the tie or handkerchief – strong colours against black just look cheap. Royal blue or cerulean are great for casual suits or blazers, but avoid them for business wear. In general, the paler and brighter a colour the more casual it is, so if you want to smarten up a linen suit commission, for instance, go for navy rather than royal blue.

Get a paler grey

Most of this applies to greys as well. Too many men wear grey that is very dark, looking more like black with a little texture to it. In fact, there are really two clear categories of grey that can be worn for business: charcoal and mid-grey.

Charcoal is a great shade for business and works particularly well in flannel, but (like navy) it cannot be mistaken for black. Of all the suit colours, however, mid-grey is the kindest on the skin tones of most men – it complements a good tan, but it doesn't wash out the pasty faced. It is for that reason that I would recommend men creating a business wardrobe (or commissioning their first bespoke suits) to start with in navy, charcoal and mid-grey.

Mid-grey is a touch lighter than the grey suit you would instinctively buy. Don't be afraid – it will look perfectly serious with a blue shirt, dark tie and deep-brown Oxfords. But then it will also work wonderfully in a casual summer setting, with a white shirt, tan shoes and perhaps a white linen handkerchief.

Other colours

A man's next commission should be a blue blazer, and you shouldn't switch to other colours until your wardrobe includes a chalk stripe, a double-breasted, a Prince-of-Wales check and a three-piece.

When you do venture into other colours, the key ones are brown and green. This seems rather daring

» How to pick fabric

There are two common mistakes men make when picking a cloth for their first bespoke suit. The first is the design: it is tempting to choose a fancy pattern and a strong colour, when as an investment in time and money it's best to look to something more conservative with your first suit.

Second is the quality of fabric. Most bespoke virgins have been schooled in ready to wear, and make the mistake that the lighter the weight and softer the look the better the quality. Although a good tailoring house can work with most fabrics, something with a bit of substance and reasonable weight will always tailor and perform best. Do take on board your tailor's advice.

As one's first bespoke suit will be different in fit and cut to what you are used to, keep the design simple. Something plain to establish a cornerstone for your wardrobe, such as a Huddersfield fine worsted in an 11 or 12 ounce weight.

until you look at tweed, the casual attire of traditional English dress and pretty much always dominant in either green or brown. Both can work in suits or jackets in any material, but remember that lighter colours and stronger colours are more casual. So in a suit, both brown and green should have a touch of the grey about them, and they should be dark enough not to dazzle.

UNIQUE » RARE » LITTLE-KNOWN » ULTIMATE **Snob**

Double button holes Traditional bespoke suits should always have two buttonholes in the lapels of a double-breasted suit. They have evolved from military dress jackets, when these would have been working buttonholes and buttoned across the chest in the same way that the other buttons down the forepart do. Indeed for a long time military dress jackets were designed with two foreparts that folded back and buttoned down on themselves – so that if unbuttoned they would have formed a double-breasted with a very large overlap. The lapel, of course, would have been of a slightly different shape, as it would otherwise have been uncomfortable under the chin. The peak that we have today on the lapel is an exaggeration of the shape of old military jackets.

Understanding cloth and material

When it comes to suit cloths, the material you know is called worsted. That's what 99 per cent of the ready-to-wear suits are made of. It's wool that has been smoothed in the yarn and again in its interlacing, to produce a smooth, clean finish. There are many different types of worsted – serge and gabardine are both worsteds yet feel very different – but again, this is a tiny proportion of the cloth on offer.

Within worsted, there are weights to suit every occasion – most of the suits you will be used to from the peg are lightweight, between 9 and 11 ounces. That's a shame, because a man should have variation and even a 14-ounce suit doesn't have to be packed away for the whole of the summer months. There will be chill days when it feels good to slip on a heavier suit, and in a plain grey or navy the trousers may be particularly useful, as trousers are cooler to wear than jackets.

So try to have a good scattering of weights between 9 and 13 in your wardrobe. If this is your first bespoke suit, you'll probably need something at the heavier end of the spectrum, as the ready to wear suits are lighter. That is a blessing, for heavier cloths hang and retain their shape better than lighter ones, so the suit will look even better for it.

Flannel

Heavier cloth is a great opportunity to wear flannel. This is a slightly less processed and therefore hairier material than worsted. It will feel slightly softer and spongier, but hangs wonderfully and is a great contrast to the shine of a silk tie and polished shoes. You may also prefer woven ties with worsted suits, to continue that contrast.

Commission a single-breasted grey flannel suit in 12- or 13-ounce cloth and see how it feels to you. Some men prefer it to anything else, as it has such character, and they spend the summer wearing 9-ounce versions that aren't strictly speaking flannel but have that same soft handle. Others only wear it in autumn and winter and – much like the Italians with suede shoes – feel that there is something about those seasons that suits greater texture. Either way one or two flannel suits are a necessity in any well-dressed man's wardrobe.

Plain tweed

Time was, a man would wear largely tweed or linen at the weekend, as the dignity of business necessitated sleeker cloths during the week. Now in many offices round the world, a man is smart if he wears a jacket of any material. A sharply cut jacket in grey Donegal tweed is still a lot smarter than a sweater, so knowing how to wear tweed, linen and all the various incarnations of cotton is important.

Tweed is felted or roughly finished wool that is woven with several differently dyed yarns. It is not just checked wool, as some manufacturers would have you believe. Indeed, the most interesting tweeds are usually not checked, but distinguished for the number of bright colours combined into a subtle overall tone.

Harris tweeds have to be woven on the Scottish Isle of Harris, though the production is much curtailed since the takeover by Brian Haggas of two of the mills there a few years ago. Tweed of the Harris type generally has one overall colour but many variegated yarns, as described above. Donegal tweed, from that region of Ireland, is distinct in having bigger flecks of a secondary colour, such as yellow in green or

Super numbers

As with bespoke details like working buttonholes, the 'super' number of a suit used to be something that men spent their time boasting about. The higher the number, the more exclusive it was.

Super 100s are a measurement of the quality of the wool. It was originally how many centimetres the yarn could be stretched to – so a super-100 wool could be stretched a metre – but has now been codified to refer to the diameter of the wool measured in microns. Most suits are between super 100 and 120. Higher numbers are sleeker and smoother but, being finer, they don't wear as well.

As a rule of thumb, until your wardrobe is so full that you only wear a suit once every month, stick with super 100s to 130s.

white in grey, and is less commonly patterned. Best to start with a classic green Harris tweed for a jacket: single breasted, slanted pockets and probably three buttons. Often the style is of the old hacking used for horse riding, hence it will have a relatively high waist button and a long centre vent.

Do, however, consider a plainer or somewhat more conservative colour for office or general city wear. Grey, pale blue or a very dark green can look just as smart as some worsteds, if cut well and with fewer bright yarns in the mix. Worsted rarely works as an odd jacket, and a cashmere blazer might seem too obvious – in that scenario smart tweed is by far the best choice.

Linen for the summer

Linen is the king of summer cloths and for good reason. It is absorbent and dries quickly, taking moisture away from the skin. It is usually in a looser weave than most wools or cottons and therefore allows more air through it. And in heavier weights it doesn't wrinkle and rumple as much as other materials, making it still relatively smart: aim for 13 or 14 ounces.

Linen is most usually made up for suitings in cream, tan and blue. You may feel that tan is only really appropriate for garden parties or strolling around town on the sunniest of days, in which case go for blue. Navy may look as if you are just wearing a rumpled business suit, so something a little brighter is recommended.

Cashmere

Cashmere is the wintery down from the hircus goat of Mongolia, combed from the animals before it falls off naturally in the spring. It is finer than normal wools and so softer, though it is best suited to separate jackets or overcoats – in a full suit cashmere would be heavy and, being soft, not drape as well. Vicuña is from small and rare camel-like creatures. It is even finer, making it very soft but a little sleek as well, and is best kept for luxurious overcoats.

Alternative options

There are some other, minor cloth options you may like to choose from:

Mohair is the hair of the angora goat, lightweight but with a slight sheen. This makes it cool but sometimes flashy. Mohair mixes can get the best of both worlds.

Hopsack is a loose weave of worsted wool that is therefore more textured but also breathable. Good for blazers.

Fresco is a patented formulation of worsted wool that is open and lightweight.

Gabardine is a tight twill in wool, cotton or anything else. Good for trousers or a nice alternative to linen in a summer suit.

Seersucker is a ribbed cotton cloth popular only in the US. Best to avoid except as a summer jacket.

Patterns and surface detail

If you're commissioning your first suit, make it plain.
There's enough to worry about with fit, style and
colour, don't chuck pattern into the mix as well. But
then, plain is rarely plain with worsted wools.
There's nailhead and pick-and-pick, both of which
most men would just describe as plain, and even
some herringbone patterns are so fine that men don't
notice them.

In general, a little surface detail is a good
thing. Unless the desired look is ultra-smooth and
sleek, texture adds to the interest of a suit and
contrasts nicely with the shine of a tie, so consider
those little patterns to be nothing more than surface
texture. Herringbone is often a good option:
essentially a broken twill, it looks always and
everywhere sophisticated.

Pinstripe   Chalkstripe

Simple, long stripes

Next are stripes. Most you see these days are pinstripe – a thin line of white or similarly pale colour that contrasts with the background. It's easy to see how to go wrong here – the stripes shouldn't be too strong or too far apart as both appear rakish and that's not a good thing, in business at least. Equally, though, the stripe should not be so dense as to be nothing more than surface detail. It's such a waste.

Stripes should always be vertical and should match at the back of the collar and bottom of the pocket flaps. They give an impression of height and therefore flatter short men. Unless you are freakishly tall, though, they will not look bad on a big man. The lengthening effect is far greater than the slimming one – in the end, a fat man in stripes just necessitates more stripes. It enables the viewer to almost measure how wide he is.

Another popular stripe is chalk. This is wider but usually used on flannel, creating a fuzziness to the

Prince of Wales plaid

Windowpane

line that is both classic and flattering. Try it on a mid-blue suit and team it with sober accessories. Not rakish, but certainly full of personality.

Checks

The king of the check is the Glenurquhart plaid, often reduced to simply glen plaid. This is a check of several overlapping lines that was made famous by Edward VII, who created his own version when he was Prince of Wales. The Duke of Windsor also popularised it during his travels to the US.

At its faintest, this check is mere surface interest, at its strongest, it is old-fashioned sportswear and unsuitable for business. The difference is really in the tone of the grey (or occasionally blue) that it is set against. Start with a mid-grey and then experiment.

The real fun though, is the overchecks. This is a simple, single line that follows the undercheck but outlines it, adding a subtle touch of colour to the pattern. Blue is standard and safe, lime green is surprisingly popular and pink also pops up now and again, but the king is a rusty orange. Try it on your fifth suit.

Lastly, there are windowpane checks. A simple pattern created by single lines, this plaid can again vary enormously in its effect from anonymity to recklessness. It is harder to do well than a Prince of Wales. A good idea would be to start with a large but faint windowpane on a charcoal ground, perhaps with a peak lapel to echo a little of the rake.

» Before bespoke

Judging the quality of a suit

Price doesn't necessarily indicate anything about the quality of a ready-to-wear suit any more. It's much more indicative of market positioning, branding and a manufacturer's broader costs. But if you're wandering round a shop and want to subtly check the quality of a suit's construction, there are a few easy ways to do so.

Floating canvas

First, and most important, check whether the suit's canvas is floating or fused. Every suit will have a layer of wool or horsehair in the chest, to give it substance and structure. This can either be stitched to the inside of the suit, or glued. The latter is cheaper and simpler, but prevents the canvas moulding to the shape of your chest. It can also bubble up under the lapels when wet.

To tell whether the canvas is floating or fused, hold the jacket around the waist button, one hand pinching the inside and one the outside. When you

» **A floating canvas** is only tacked at the edges, so is flexible and moulds easily.

pull the two apart, you should be able to feel the canvas in between. If you can't, it has been fused to the front.

Sleeveheads and armholes

Second, check the armholes. For a suit to fit well, the armhole should be small but the sleevehead big. This stops the body of the suit from being yanked around when you move your arms. A big, looser armhole forces you to drag the rest of your jacket with you as you move your arm. A larger sleevehead allows for a natural shape at the top of the sleeve despite the small opening. If the difference in the two sizes is very big, the sleeve has to be attached by hand.

To check this, put on the jacket and see how tight the fit is under your armpit. And try moving your arm, checking how much it drags the body with it.

Hand-sewn touches

Finally, good suits have their buttonholes sewn by hand. This is largely aesthetic – it makes almost no practical difference to longevity or ease of use. But it does indicate greater time and effort put into the finishing touches.

Ready-to-wear sizes

Understanding sizing is key to getting the most out of ready to wear (RTW). The sizes go back more than 100 years. Hart Schaffner & Marx (now famous worldwide for dressing President Barack Obama) was the first to produce proportioned suits in 1906. It analysed the male body and broke it down into generic sizes – tall, short, stout and thin.

Standardised sizes

Later, that was refined to categorisation by the size of a man's chest. Hence our current system of 38 inches, 40 inches, 42 inches, etc. The standard had to be about the jacket, as it is so much harder to alter than the trousers, and the chest is the most consistent part of the jacket.

The waist and length of the trousers, though, were also based on this system. The standard 'drop' today – the difference between a suit's chest measurement and its trouser waist – is 6 inches. So, generally speaking, a 40-inch jacket comes with 34-inch trousers.

If you spend enough time researching RTW suits, and have two or three points altered, it shouldn't be hard to find a good fit. It will never compare to the sculpted look of bespoke, but the suit will fit well – probably better than at least 70 per cent of the male population, which never bothers with either research or alterations.

Trying on a suit

If RTW is what you want, or is all you can afford, you will need to have parts of it altered. To know what needs to be altered – indeed, to know whether it's worth buying the suit in the first place – you will need to be able to analyse all aspects of fit. So here's a rundown. This will also come in useful in the book when we discuss bespoke fittings.

Unfortunately jackets are not simple pieces of tailoring. The way the cloth looks across your back, for example, is affected by everything from the angle of the shoulder seam to the slope of your shoulders, and your natural posture to the height of the waist button. It is not just a question of doing it up and making sure you can breathe.

The fit at the waist

Start with the waist. Fasten the waist button and only the waist button (the middle one on a three-button suit, top on a two-button and I think you can figure out a one-button). This is the fulcrum that the whole jacket has been designed on, anchoring the shoulders and revealing the jacket's structure.

Tug at that button slightly and see how much excess there is. An inch or two is fine. You don't want any stretch lines radiating from the button when it is fastened; but equally it should not be too loose. Unlike a shirt, say, you will undo this button when you sit down (unless the jacket is double-breasted) so the jacket's waist can follow yours quite closely.

» Size matters

Many brands and designers subtly tweak the shape
they label '40' every season, usually based on fit
models hired exclusively for that. Also, given that a
40-inch chest can come in long, regular or short, two
or three different styles per line, two or more lines
per brand, across many different brands, there are
actually hundreds of 40s out there to choose from.

Sizes vary across different continents to account for
variations in size among the population. There are
also variations within sub-brands. Ralph Lauren's
Black Label, for instance, was launched with a
seven-inch drop, presuming its prospective clients to
be more athletic than Polo or Purple Label. The latter
now also has a Custom Fit category, which also
translates as a larger drop. As the drop is reflected in
the jacket's waist as well as the trousers, a Black
Label or Custom Fit jacket is also slimmer.

Check the lengths

Next, look at the length of the jacket. There are many ways to assess whether this is correct, including if it matches your inside leg. But there are two simple and effective ways. Is the length of the jacket (from shoulder to jacket hem) roughly half the height of the whole suit (from shoulder to trouser hem). And, secondly, does the jacket finish about

Trying on a suit

The neck and »
shoulders are
key to the fit
of the suit.

The jacket »
should end
half way
down your
hands.

« The waist
button is the
fulcrum of
the jacket.

« The length of
the jacket
should be half
the height of
the suit.

halfway down your hands, so you can curl your fingers under it? Compare these two rules, and as long as they are both close, the jacket fits.

Of course, many of these points are subject to taste and fashion. Recently the trend has been towards shorter, 'bumfreezer' jackets that recall the 1960 Beatles-era. That's fine if it's what you want, but use these guidelines so you can tell if the jacket is of this style so at least you're making an informed decision.

The arms of the jacket should finish around your wrist bone – the point from which your hand flexes. If your shirt finishes at the base of the thumb, this should leave around half an inch of cuff showing (try to wear shirts that fit you well when trying on a suit, if possible).

Neck and shoulders

Most important to the fit of a suit, though, is the neck and shoulders as they are the hardest to get altered. The neck should sit flush on your collar when you are standing naturally (not dead straight like you are on parade). If it stands away, the collar needs to be tightened; if it is against the neck but there are stretch marks below the collar, it needs to be loosened.

Finally, if the shoulders fit, then the jacket's sleeve should just touch the muscle of your shoulder as it flows down the arm. Your shoulder should not create a bulge in the cloth, but nor should the sleeve hang loose beyond it. It should just touch.

Alterations tailors

Once you've bought the suit, go to the alterations tailor. This isn't a specialist group – for most places in the world today, particularly the US, it is all tailors. Try and find a good one though.

Alterations tailors regularly shorten the length of trousers and take in the waist. The first doesn't even require the opening of a seam; the second is a simple opening of the waist seam at the back for a few inches, and closing up.

Waist alterations

They will also regularly have clients that want the waist taken in on their jacket. Most ready-to-wear suits are made deliberately larger than average in this department. That alteration requires the two side seams on the jacket to be opened – which means unpicking the lining and making sure they get the angle of the alteration even as it narrows towards the scye (armhole) and the hip. But it is a regular procedure and not that technically demanding.

Jacket sleeves

Next on the sliding scale of difficulty is probably shortening the jacket's arms. This can be done one of two ways – either from the cuff or from the shoulder. The latter is far harder as it means detaching the sleeve, shortening it and reattaching, but it is the only option if the jacket has working buttons on the cuff. If the buttons are purely decorative, the sleeve can be shortened from the cuff and the bottom button simply shifted to the top of the row to retain the look.

So this is technically more difficult, and should be something you think about twice if the jacket is a bespoke or high-grade Italian one. Both are more likely to have a sleevehead that is substantially larger than the armhole it goes into, so the alterations tailor will have to repeat the process of easing in the excess material when he replaces your sleeves. This is not something to be trusted to someone whose prime business is dry cleaning, but while this requires a good amount of skill, it does not require much artistry. The tailor is simply attempting to rewind and then redo an existing process.

Adjustments to neck and shoulders

Altering the neck and shoulders is different – it's a case of figuration. This is the term for modelling a suit to your physique. Not simply getting the measurements right, but knowing how to pitch the sleeve differently to cope with your posture, or allow more fullness on one side of the back to deal with a prominent shoulder blade.

When a tailor cuts the length of the collar of your suit, so it fits more snugly on your neck, he has the potential to alter all the figuration. Opening the back seam can unbalance one side or the other, pull the front parts of the jacket apart or ruin the pitch of the sleeve so that it hangs forward from your body.

For a good tailor, it is not difficult. But there aren't many of those around. To be safe, as mentioned earlier, always make sure the suit you buy off the rack fits well on the neck and shoulders.

Made to measure

Made to measure will always be a much better fit for you than RTW, with many more options to adjust the size to your body. It can drop the shoulders if yours droop; it can narrow the trousers if you prefer a tighter fit; it can even alter the width of the sleeves to cope with particularly bulging biceps. The fit won't be able to cope with one protruding hip, a slightly prominent shoulder blade or a slight stoop that throws the body forward and ever-so-slightly to the right. But it will fit very well. It will probably fit you better than 95 per cent of the suits out there fit their owners. It isn't quite bespoke, but it's damn good.

A taste of design

One of the other advantages of MTM over RTW, is that it gives you a little taste of design. Many customers originally seek out bespoke for the superiority of fit, but their interest is maintained by the possibility of design, personal expression and inflicting their personality on the world through the medium of bespoke suiting.

With most MTM orders you will be able to pick the colour and type of the wool, the material of the buttons, the shape of the lapels and the colour of the lining. You will be able to specify the number of pockets, vents and pleats, not to mention cuffs, breasts and buttons. To those with a fascination for men's clothing, this is sorely tempting.

Increasing popularity

MTM has become increasingly popular in recent years, with many high-street brands that you wouldn't otherwise associate with tailoring introducing the service. This is essentially an easy way for them to jump on the bandwagon of a tailoring revival. As men become interested again in how their jackets fit, they want more than a standard block. MTM enables the brands to offer a little more – using the same fabrics, the same trimmings and perhaps even the same factory that produces their normal suits. The additional manpower is minimal, it just needs a certain number with enough expertise to get the measuring right (too many brands fall down on this point – if you've ever tried out a mail-order suit service where you or a friend has to take your measurements, you'll know how hard it can be).

Staying with a brand

Returning to the point about design, the advantage of this growth in high-street MTM is that customers can still get the style and cut they like from the brand they like. New companies or tailors are a risk; men like to stick with what they know. UK high-street brand Reiss, for example, has very distinctive suits: usually with a mix of mohair or subtle takes on flannel, and in a slim, contemporary cut. It introduced MTM in 2010, at about a 30 per cent mark-up on RTW. For someone who wants to upgrade their wardrobe while staying with a look they know, and for those who would rather wait four weeks than eight, MTM is ideal.

Words from the wise

Antonio de Matteis
CEO, Kiton, Italy

» Not all tailoring is bespoke

Ready-to-wear clothes are the bulk of Kiton's business. On our shirts all the buttonholes are hand-sewn; the collars are unfused and the lining exposed on the inside-back; all the seams are sewn by hand (except the edge of the collar).

On a jacket, all the seams are hand-sewn except the centre seam up the back. Hand stitches permit greater movement. This is particularly important around the shoulder and collar, where the arm and neck move against the cloth. The same is true of the puckering in the cloth at the shoulder seam, where the sleeve enters an armhole that is almost 30 per cent smaller. There's also a roll of padding sewn around the armhole of our jackets with thick basting, to make sure that shirt-like Neapolitan shoulder doesn't lose its shape through ironing.

The whole jacket has quilting stitches running around its edge to give it greater body. This is tailoring, but it isn't bespoke. There's a difference.

Directory of retailers

There are some wonderful ready-to-wear suit makers out there. Their value is largely in design and cloth, aspects of the suit on which bespoke tailors will always struggle to compete with the top designers. But having recommended 'designers' quite broadly, I would advise you to always avoid the catwalk type unless aesthetics are your only consideration. Construction-wise, they will nearly always be the worst value for money.

Among the better RTW suit makers are Kiton, Brioni and Tom Ford. All very expensive but of wonderful quality. A little tip: most of these brands will have their cloths made by the same mills that bespoke tailors use. Just find out which mills and which lines. They may not be exactly the same, but they will be very close. Then you can have a bespoke version made.

These seven brands may seem like a small number. But if you remove all the high fashion (some well-made but never worth the money on quality alone) and the High Street brands, there are few good ones left. If I had to narrow down this list and shop for my own wardrobe, I would probably opt for a summer jacket from Rubinacci, a blazer from Loro Piana and a tuxedo from Tom Ford. Ralph Lauren would be inspiration.

Brioni

Flagship store: 50 Via Barberini, Rome
Tel: +39 06 4620 161

www.brioni.com

Also has branches in London, Tokyo, New York and a handful of other places outside Italy. Long famous as the Italian luxury house that clothed James Bond, Brioni is not for the faint-hearted. Its prices for suits regularly top those of the most expensive bespoke tailoring establishments, over the Savile Row standard of £3000. The quality of the workmanship is extremely high, with many aspects like buttonholes being sewn by hand, as well as the collars and sleeves being attached by hand. But the amount of handwork is never going to be as high as the bespoke tailors – rather, Brioni and similar Italian houses like Kiton pride themselves on the most luxurious materials possible.

Kiton

Flagship and showroom: 11 Via Gesu, Milan
Tel: +39 02 7639 0240

www.kiton.it/

Although less well-known outside Italy than Brioni, Kiton is just as luxurious and no less expensive. Specialising particularly in ultra-lightweight worsted cloths and fine cashmeres, its style is typically Neapolitan: soft jackets with a lot of drape, with little structure or canvas; shoulders are natural and often inset (sleeve sewn underneath the shoulder, like a shirt). This contrasts with the more classic and Roman shape of Brioni. Kiton is also well-known for its bright colours in summer and experiments in cloth and tone – Autumn/Winter 2010 featured an unstructured green jacket made from a stretchable, jersey cloth. Stores in 11 countries.

Tom Ford

Flagship store: 845 Madison Avenue, New York.
Tel: +1 212 359 0300.

www.tomford.com

Le Snob ESSENTIAL The biggest arrival in luxury menswear for 20 years. Once Tom Ford launched his eponymous label on leaving Gucci, he quickly became famous in the industry for researching the very highest possible qualities of cloths and manufacturing possible, from one-piece leather jackets to hand-cut suits. The price tags are big and aspirational and the cuts aren't for everyone – they are masculine, big-shouldered and big-lapelled. The patterns too are strong and hard to pull off. But the quality and mastery of colour and tone is superb, and this

Tom Ford classic tuxedo »

would be the place to go for a tuxedo. Dozens of stores worldwide, sprung up in double-quick time.

Loro Piana

Flagship store: 27C Via Montenapoleone, Milan.
Tel: +39 02 7772901.

www.loropiana.com

Le Snob ESSENTIAL Luxurious casualwear for the off-duty Italian. Loro Piana is famed for its cashmere, becoming the first house in the world to offer baby cashmere a few years ago – combed from the young goats in their first Spring, it produces a tiny amount of wool that is two microns finer than normal cashmere. Like Zegna, Loro Piana has also done much to protect the vicuña camelids in South America. The company produces knitwear and blazers, as well as all manner of other clothing items and accessories (and its own cloths for tailors, at least as fine as Zegna). Watch out for the Storm System label in some items – this is a wind- and rain-proofing fabric patented by Loro

« **Loro Piana** blazer in baby cashmere

Piana and often used by other brands. A few dozen stores worldwide.

Ermenegildo Zegna

Flagship store: 27E Via Montenapoleone, Milan
Tel: +39 02 7600 6437

www.zegna.com

As a cloth manufacturer, the house of Zegna is virtually unsurpassed in all the world. It still makes most of its money out of supplying cloths to other tailors, or making suits with those cloths for brands like Tom Ford. Its retail offering is very mixed. At the bottom end it competes with the likes of Canali and Corneliani. At the top end it makes pieces that compare with the big Italian luxury names for handwork. Make sure you know which you're getting. There are hundreds of stores worldwide, in every major city, and in 27 of the 50 US states.

Rubinacci

Flagship store: 26 Via Filangieri., Naples
Tel: +39 081 415 793

www.marianorubinacci.net

 A Neapolitan tailoring house that has become famous for its use of colour – particularly as worn by the third generation of the family, Luca Rubinacci, in his regular appearances on Scott Schuman's blog The Sartorialist. Rubinacci offers bespoke tailoring around the world (as do Brioni and Kiton) but is increasingly well known outside Italy for its accessories and ready to wear. Luca launched a range of ready to wear and accessories for the first time in Autumn/Winter

2010. (While Kiton and Brioni offer bespoke, it makes up a small part of their overall business. A greater proportion is made to measure.) Also has stores in New York, London, Tokyo and in Italy, Rome and Milan.

Ralph Lauren

Flagship store: Rhinelander mansion, 867
Madison Avenue, New York. Tel: +1 212 606 2100

www.ralphlauren.com

Simply the most consistent purveyor of the classic American style there has ever been. And by classic American, we mean everything English with American inspiration thrown in. Polo, but with Long-Island arrogance. Ralph Lauren's quality too, is often very high – even Polo suits usually feature loose sewing of the linings, something few other mid-range suits bother with. As with Zegna, there is a lot of variation in retail though. Learn the difference between Polo, Black and Purple labels – the last one is what you really want. Hundreds of stores around the world.

» The bespoke process

Getting measured

Having clothes made by a tailor can be a frustrating business. Truth is, few of us are any good at designing clothes. That's what makes the retail experience satisfying: browsing designs and being inspired by something that we love but would never have imagined. Other people design for us.

However, once you know all the elements of fabric, style and pattern you're in a much better position than most. You know how many buttons you want on your jacket and why, which type of wool and in which weight. All that's left is to master the fitting process itself. Get it right and you'll bespeak something as good as retail. After two or three attempts, you'll create something better.

First steps

Usually, a tailor will discuss cloth with you first, before getting out the measuring tape. Little details like pockets and buttons may come later, but he'll want to get a sense of the weight and style of suit first. A Norfolk jacket fits differently to a sharp, navy worsted.

Then, on with the measuring. Once the tailor gets going, the number of measurements may seem bewildering. On the trousers, for example, he'll need the inside and outside leg on each side; the waist, hips and seat; and then the thigh, knee and cuff. And the jacket is much more complicated. Just stand still and let him do his job – but bear a few of the following things in mind.

» Your first bespoke suit

When you visit a bespoke tailor for the first time, make sure to wear a suit you feel comfortable in. Your favourite suit is a great starting point and gives the tailor an idea of both fit and style. Or if you have a particular style in mind, bring in a photo or a previous suit as a reference.

The first step will be to gauge the best kind of cloth to use. This will usually be dictated by the intended function of the suit. When talking to the cutter, the key is honesty. Not only does dialogue establish your needs quickly and accurately, it also helps you relax, showing your true posture, which will be discreetly noted by the cutter.

If anything, communication is even more vital at the first fitting. That establishes the details of the suit and has the customer's individual style incorporated into this plain baste. It's an important time to speak up with any concerns or doubts about fit or design details.

Stand naturally

First, stand naturally. One of the greatest arts of tailoring is arranging the back parts so they fit smoothly all the way up your back, resting evenly across your shoulders and fitting snugly against the back of your neck. No off-the-peg suit will do this. It will always be a little too tight or loose at the neck and rest unevenly on one shoulder. This is because off-the-peg suits are made for an average stance, with no lean forward or back and neither to one side or the other.

And no one is average. Everyone stoops a little bit; everyone has one shoulder that drops slightly more than the other. So don't try to hide this from the tailor, stand as naturally as you can, and try to relax. Shake your arms out; roll your neck; take a breath, and let go. Then try to stay in that frame of mind for the next 15 minutes or so.

Talk to your tailor

Second thing to remember: anticipate the aspects of fit that the tailor will not know from looking at you. How long do you like your sleeves? It helps if you wear a shirt that you like the fit of – then he can refer to the amount of exposed cuff rather than to your wrist bone. How long do you like your trousers? Again, wear something you are already quite satisfied with.

The beauty of bespoke is that there will be at least three more occasions after this for you to express your feelings on tightness and looseness. And it's much easier to give your opinion on an actual jacket than in the abstract. So just give some rough indicators to the tailor. Grunt approval, shrug or wrinkle your nose. He should get the message.

The basted fitting

The next stage is the basted fitting. This may be anywhere from three weeks to two months after the initial appointment, depending on the business of the tailor and – frankly – his attitude to taking on new work. Some tailors work harder when there's more business; others take on more staff; some just let the time between fittings drag out.

In those three weeks, the cutter that measured you up will have cut a series of paper patterns approximating the pattern of your suit – front and back panels, sleeves, collar and trousers. He will then either have cut out the wool himself – by laying a pattern onto two layers of the cloth – or given it to a 'striker' (undercutter) to do so.

A basting tailor will then roughly sew all the pieces together. The lines are not rough, but the stitch

« **Paper pattern**
for a suit
jacket.

are long and loose, so that after your basted fitting they can be ripped out and the cloth re-cut.

Trying it on

Putting on a basted jacket is a slightly odd feeling. It doesn't look like the suit you envisaged. It has no structure, has white stitches all over it and, perhaps most distractingly, may only have one arm. Do not panic. The basted fitting is all about fit, not style.

If your tailor is any good, he will spend most of his time looking and marking, rather than asking questions. He's analysing how the cloth falls across your back, deciding that one or other shoulder has to be a little lower, that there is too much drape under the arm or that the collar has to be higher. Alterations will be chalked on, for the guidance of his shears later on.

From your point of view, consider the elements of fit you can see. Is the sleeve you do have too long or too short? The tailor will have pinned the front of the jacket closed at the waist – does this feel too tight or too loose? Remember to move a little (when he is not about to pin or chalk you). A jacket should be comfortable when you are walking and stretching, not just standing still. It is not made of lycra.

« **Trying on the suit** at the basted fitting.

Basted stage construction

It's easiest to tell how a suit is put together when you see it at the basted stage. That first fitting shows the various parts of the jacket – two back parts, two foreparts, collar and the front and back of sleeves – sewn loosely together so the tailor can get an idea of the fit and then easily take it apart again to be re-cut.

Those are the outer parts. Then you have the lining to the body and the sleeves. It is usually made today of Bemberg (rayon) or Emerzine (viscose), these allow the wearer to slip the jacket on and off easily. Other than perhaps some slight insulation and structure, that is their sole purpose. The sleeve lining will usually be white with alternating coloured lines, no matter what the lining of the body. Some tailors have house patterns for the sleeve that they always use and can identify their work.

Canvassing

When men (and their tailors) talk about unstructured suits, one of the things they mean is a reduction in the lining in the jacket. But they also mean a suit with less internal structure to the chest.

Within the chest there will be one, two or three layers of felt, wool, cotton or horsehair in some combination. A standard English suit will have a layer of horsehair running all the way behind the forepart of the suit, with a layer of felt in the upper half. Those two are sewn loosely together with basting stitches and then attached, again loosely – though securely – all the way around the edge.

The horsehair most resembles a thin layer of canvas, and the entire structure is usually referred to as the 'canvassing' of the chest. It is very flexible, stretches and moulds easily. So it will shape to the contours of your chest after a few wears, creating a three-dimensional shape that fits you in a way the tailor cannot build for. This 3-D shape is one of the reasons it is important to hang, press and pack your jacket carefully.

Because the felt and horsehair is only tacked at the edges, it can move or 'float' within the suit. This is the floating canvas that is referred to as the hallmark of a good suit. Poorer products will glue (fuse) the canvas to the forepart, reducing its ability to move and mould (see page 42).

Variations on structure

More layers and different materials can be used to create greater shape to the jacket. In the opposite direction, it can be cut down in size or removed altogether to reduce structure. The unlined suits discussed above obviously do not contain any canvas. Half-lined suits usually do, but even fully lined suits can just have canvas down to the waist, in order to reduce weight and make the jacket more breathable.

Coats equally – it is rare to find coats today that are fully lined, right down to the hem. It is one reason that vintage coats tend to be so much heavier. It makes them much more wind-resistant though.

Other structural elements

Other structural aspects of the suit include the collar and shoulders. The collar is pretty similar to the chest – a layer of canvas and one of melton, sewn loosely together and then attached to the back of the neck. There is more variation in the shoulders, though they will tend to follow the same philosophy as the chest. So an Anderson & Sheppard-style suit will have less shoulder padding or, at the least, it will be of a softer, spongier material.

The wadding at the top of the sleevehead (the shoulder of the suit beyond the seam that attaches it to the sleeve) can also vary. More wadding creates a 'roped' shoulder that stands higher – giving the impression that there is a strip of rope running around the shoulder. Extreme versions and padding can lead to a 'pagoda' shoulder that actually curve up, leaving the line of the wearer's shoulder entirely.

De-structured suit

When Giorgio Armani famously de-structured the suit in the late seventies, he both reduced the weight of the canvas and cut it down in size (as well as making the whole suit baggier). Italian tailors had been doing it for years, driven by the need to cope with higher temperatures than those in England. Most Italian suits today will tend to have less structuring. It's easy to tell how much canvas there is and how far it stretches – just pinch the forepart on front and back and feel the layer in between.

» Soft versus structured

Tailors like Anderson & Sheppard on Old
Burlington Street in London use two layers of lighter
weight wool or cotton, to soften their suits. Equally
prestigious Huntsman on Savile Row is famous for a
more 'structured' look and uses a thicker canvas.

Proponents of the former approach (including
Steven Hitchcock, son of A&S's head cutter John
Hitchcock, and ex-A&S cutter Thomas Mahon)
would say their suits are more comfortable.
Proponents of the latter (including ex-Huntsman head
cutters Richard Anderson and Terry Haste) would say
theirs flatter the customer more.

Each is merely a question of taste. If you want a
comparison, all are usually open to going into the
shop to try on or at least see standard garments.
(Indeed Huntsman also offers ready to wear, so there
is a ready selection of models to try.)

The forward fitting

At the next fitting, often called the forward, the most obvious things that will be missing are the buttons and buttonholes. This is because any alterations that have to be made at this stage are much easier if buttonholes have not already been cut. If one sleeve has to be shortened, for example, it can be done by taking cloth off the end; if the buttonholes were already sewn, the sleeve would have to be detached from the shoulder and shortened at that end.

The forward fitting is the first time you will see your suit in something approaching a finished form. You will be able to see how the design is going to work, how much space will be left for the tie and where the gorge (the seam between the collar and lapel) will sit.

Assessing the fit

Look the suit up and down and consider every aspect. Are you happy with the jacket length? Are the pockets the right height and straight/slant? Is the waist tight enough, does it flare too much into the skirt? The forward fitting is meant to avoid any alterations on the finished suit, so your tailor should be happy you're spotting so many things at this stage.

Of course, far more important is that the tailor pick up any last points of fit, such as the balance across the shoulders and line through the waist. Changes should be minimal and final. Your pattern will be altered to incorporate these, so that in the long term a suit is nearly perfect as soon as it is cut and you can skip at least one of these fittings (see page 75).

Final alterations

A few weeks later, you should have the finished suit. Still think of this as a fitting, though, especially if it is your first from this tailor. Don't go to the appointment expecting to walk away with your suit. Chances are there will be something small you don't like, and much better to pipe up now then come back with the suit in a week or so.

Common things that often need changing at this stage are the length of sleeves and trousers. Something about the other alterations made after the forward fitting always seems to tweak one or both of those. And both lengths are crucial to a well-fitting suit.

The finished suit

So after another week or two, you should have your finished suit. But again, don't think about this as the end of the process. As you wear the jacket it will mould to your chest and fidget until it sits naturally on your neck. This may mean that after five or six outings the neck becomes a little tight or a little loose. This is not the fault of the tailor – he cannot know these things without seeing how a suit wears on you in reality.

Go back, get these little things seen to somewhere down the line. And bear them in mind for the next suit. It may take a long time to get to perfection, but the steps get smaller and smaller.

Words from the wise

John Hitchcock Head cutter,
Anderson & Sheppard, UK

» What is soft tailoring?

Soft tailoring means achieving comfort without sacrificing style. The shoulder padding is lighter, creating a more natural, sloping shoulder. The canvassing of the chest is lighter, making it less rigid while retaining the benefits of a fully canvassed suit.

The waist is suppressed, but gently, creating a classic and smooth silhouette. There is extra drape across the chest and shoulder blades, which adds flexibility without creating bulk. The combination of a small armhole and large sleevehead holds the chest and neck in place while allowing the arms to move naturally. It is easy and comfortable to wear.

One sign of its comfort has to be seeing myself and the other cutters and staff of Anderson & Sheppard working in it all day long. It's hard to trust a tailor that doesn't wear his own tailoring to work in.

The jacket created by soft tailoring retains all the sharpness and smartness of any other suit jacket. A cardigan it is not.

Subsequent suit commissions

Once you have commissioned a few suits similar in style from one particular tailor, you have a choice to skip either the basted or forward fitting. This is not to cut corners; rather it is the next step in bespoke, once you are happy with the shape you have achieved with one particular tailor. At this stage his pattern for, say, a single-breasted jacket on you should be pretty much cemented. The balance should work well, the sleeves will have been adjusted to just the right length and small issues like the height of the waist button have been ironed out.

So it makes sense to speed the process up. Effectively you would normally have three fittings: basted, forward and final.

Skip the basted or forward?

If you skip the basted, the cutter could send the cloth to the jacket-maker immediately, without having to wait for you to come in for a fitting. It would also save the time it takes for the jacket to be basted (say half a day). If you skip the forward fitting, the jacket maker would not have to send back his work at all, so the time saved would be slightly greater: no time waiting for you plus no lost time in couriering the jacket (twice).

Fit or design

Really though, the choice comes down to whether you are more confident in the fit of the jackets or in their design. The basted fitting is mostly about

In the details

Why hand-stitching
makes a difference

» Sew superior

The best bespoke suit will be entirely made by hand,
allowing flexibility and attention to detail in key
areas of the suit. Attaching the lining to the inside of
the suit by hand, for instance, allows it to move
when you do, without disturbing the cloth outside so
that your silhouette remains smooth and sharp. You
can tell if the lining has been done by hand by
looking at the point where it joins the bottom of the
back part. Machine stitches are tight, small and very
regular. Hand stitches may still be quite regular, but
there will be tiny variations and bigger gaps. The
shoulder seam also benefits from handwork,
allowing it to stretch slightly as you move and reach.
Hand sewing also means the tailor can use silk
thread where needed, which is stronger than the
normal cotton used by sewing machines.

Finally, with hand sewing, a large sleevehead can
be fitted into a small armhole, which allows a man
to move his arms freely without disturbing the fit of
the rest of the suit.

balance – it is the tailor's opportunity to get the figuration right and re-cut the cloth if anything is wrong. The forward fitting helps too, but it is mostly about you seeing the design in its near-finished form. It is not too late to alter the button positions or the roll of the lapel, or to spot any mistakes.

You may not be bad at designing suits, but take it as a given that your tailor is a lot better at fitting them. You may have designed perhaps a dozen or so; he's cut hundreds. So if you plan to skip one, make it the basted fitting.

UNIQUE » RARE » LITTLE-KNOWN » ULTIMATE **Snob**

The lap seam Lap seams are an anachronism that still have a few followers in bespoke circles. They were originally used to add greater strength to a join, and they are more substantial. But today they are used for style, to subtly highlight the line of the leg for example. They are generally used on the side seams of trousers and involve leaving a little flap of cloth, lying flat and facing backwards, down the seam. In a way they are an exaggerated version of a raised seam, where both pieces of cloth simply overlap and are sewn together (what you get down the inside of a pair of jeans). With a lap seam both pieces are sewn together, folded over and then sewn down, leaving a little excess cloth or 'lap'.

The fit of bespoke trousers

At some point during your first session with a tailor, he will ask you what length you like your trousers to be. While there are guidelines for this, it is also a question of taste. Give your opinion on the length, then try sitting down. Again, it is important that they are comfortable when you are moving, not just standing still. Cloth can be taut but should not constrain. Let them sit naturally on your waist, do not hike them up or down.

Standard length

The traditional length is such that the trousers fall on your shoes with no break in the crease at the back

Standard length
with a single break

Shorter length
with no break

– it is a straight, uninterrupted line from hip to heel – and in the front there is a single break (fold). This is roughly the same length as the trousers will be if you stand in your socks and the back crease just touches the floor.

This standard length will make your legs appear long and sleek, with no interruption in that elegant line at the rear and minimal disturbance at the front. It also means others are unlikely to see much of your socks as you walk along.

Shorter length

However, the trend in recent years has been for shorter trousers. While designers like Thom Browne have taken it to extreme lengths, many brands and tailors have tended towards the short – something reflected in the fashion for men to turn up the bottom of their jeans.

But short trousers are not a recent phenomenon. A particular strain of southern European men, particularly in Milan, have always worn their suit trousers short (see box). Usually they will wear their trousers so they just touch the top of their shoes – no break in the front as well as the back.

If you want to echo this tradition of shorter trousers, I recommend going for turn-ups (cuffs). It helps that they too are more fashionable than they used to be. And of course it is easy to reverse that decision later.

However, if you want something more conservative and less likely to be noticed, go for a single break in the front. Perhaps a shallow break, just to give your shoes a little breathing room.

Words from the wise

Riccardo Renzi
UK representative, Kiton, Italy

» Italian trousers

I've always liked short trousers. Though they don't really seem short to me, they seem normal.

Trousers that just touch the top of your shoes mean you can see the shoes, for a start. And I like my shoes; I want to show them off. I never saw the point of having beautiful leather shoes and covering the back half in a long, wide trouser leg. If you have monk-straps you want to see the strap, otherwise what's the point? You can understand it perhaps if you're English and all your shoes are black. But mine are brown – and so many different browns.

When some foreign men wear shorter trousers they get it wrong – the trousers aren't narrow enough, so they flap around when they walk. Shorter trousers need to be cut narrowly and have turn-ups, so they hug the calves and are weighed down by the extra material of the cuff. That way they stay there, just resting gently on the top of the shoe.

Where should trousers sit?

In my opinion, there are really only two options on the waist of your trousers – either it sits above your hip bone or in its hollow.

The first will probably require braces. This is the traditional height – it will be around the same place as your waist button on the jacket and is better with pleats (to flow out and over those hip bones). As it will be on the middle of your stomach, it is also more comfortable with braces – braces allow the waist to be a good inch wider than normal, as tension is not required to keep them up.

The second position is what 99 per cent of young men wear today. Not slack, not drooping halfway down the bottom, but sitting across the hips and definitely below the stomach. The most important thing is that the position feels natural to you and does not alter as you move around the fitting room. If it does change, the length will be ruined – and that is the part of a pair of trousers most constantly on display.

Directory of bespoke tailors

No one has tried every tailor on Savile Row. Most that can afford that level of bespoke stick with just one, and only move if their cutter leaves or retires. Some continue to patronise more than one, but they are the minority. Their experience is very limited among the 20 or so bespoke tailors on and around the Row. Once you go off Savile Row, the number doubles or triples – even more once you venture into the City. This is, of course, not counting visiting tailors that have their suits made elsewhere.

All this is a roundabout way of saying that the following list is necessarily subjective. It is built on personal experience, reputation and the many recommendations of peers. Consider this a cumulative recommendation, but no guarantee. Unfortunately for one's bank balance, the only way to truly find a tailor you love is by trial and error.

United Kingdom

The three Savile Row tailors with the biggest reputation are probably Anderson & Sheppard, Huntsman and Henry Poole. The first two have the most identifiable silhouette – both soft and hard respectively – and the last can claim to be the founder of the Row. Several scions of the first two are dotted about and do similar work, notably Stephen Hitchcock (son of Anderson & Sheppard's head cutter), Thomas Mahon (based up north and a former cutter there) and Richard Anderson (former head cutter at Huntsman's). Norton & Sons, under new owner Patrick Grant, has probably become the most progressive. Maurice Sedwell is almost unique in his reputation among his peers. Off the Row, Jonathan Quearney is recommended while, in the City, Graham Browne has a growing reputation under cutter Russell Howarth.

Anderson & Sheppard

32 Old Burlington Street, London

Tel: +44 20 7734 1420

Le Snob ESSENTIAL Known for its soft structure, Anderson & Sheppard is one of the best known names on (or very close to) the Row. Its distinctive shape is inherited from Frederick Scholte, the revolutionary tailor who pioneered soft tailoring through a more natural shoulder and lighter chest padding, cut on the bias for greater movement. Today Andersons has a following around the world, though

« **Anderson & Sheppard** jackets are reknowned for the distinctive shape of soft tailoring.

as many swear at the style as swear by it. The relatively new premises on Old Burlington Street are also among the best of any Row tailor, exuding both tradition and modern elegance. Get a feel for the style, and stick with it if you like it.

Steven Hitchcock

13 Savile Row (lower ground), London

Tel: +44 20 7287 2492

Steven Hitchcock is the son of Mr John Hitchcock, head cutter at Anderson & Sheppard and the man who has cut several superb suits for me. His son's reputation is very strong, and many visit him in his basement rooms on Savile Row for a slightly different (and slightly cheaper) take on the Anderson & Sheppard look.

Thomas Mahon

Warwick Hall, Warwick-on-Eden, Carlisle

Tel: +44 1228 561700

Another ex-Andersons cutter, Thomas Mahon, also has a site called English Cut, which developed quite a following when it was started up five years ago – one of the first of the old-school tailors to embrace this format. His cut is a soft, A&S cut and comes highly recommended. He was the Prince of Wales's tailor for over 20 years and that distinctive soft shoulder can be seen in many of Charles's double-breasteds today. I also recommend his black tie, with which Thomas is particularly emphatic on the real silk used in the jacket's facings. Being based in

Carlisle, north England, makes Thomas cheaper than anyone else on the Row, though he does most of his fitting and client appointments on the Row still. The cutting is all done in the frankly beautiful surroundings up in Cumbria.

H. Huntsman & Sons

11 Savile Row, London

Tel: +44 20 7734 7441

Le Snob ESSENTIAL Huntsman has reigned supreme at the heart of Savile Row for 160 years, in its own words. Whether it has reigned exactly is rather subjective, but it is certainly among the top few houses for tradition and reputation. The classic Huntsman shape is rather different to Anderson & Sheppard – a strong shoulder, greater padding in the chest and a nipped waist. Single-breasted jackets

The Huntsman jacket Examples of the classic jacket style, with a stronger, structured look.

usually feature a single button. It is more upright, military and to that extent, flattering than soft tailoring. But some people take against the cut. If you prefer a softer structure to a suit, the tight little stitches of Huntsman can seem a little constricting. But then devotees of the structured look would dismiss soft-tailored jackets as mere cardigans. Unlike Anderson & Sheppard, Huntsman offers both ready to wear and made to measure, so you can wander into the shop and try on a suit to get an idea of the fit.

Richard Anderson

13 Savile Row, London

Tel: +44 20 7734 0001

Richard Anderson was briefly the head cutter of Huntsman, and the youngest man to hold the position, before he left to start up his own shop down the road. His excellent book *Bespoke: Savile Row Ripped and Smoothed* tells of his career from apprentice to cutter to proprietor. No other book gives such an insight to the career of a tailor on Savile Row. The house cut is consequently similar to Huntsman, though Richard has a reputation for more adventurous styles and a glamorous clientele. Expect an openness to innovation and suggestion.

Henry Poole

15 Savile Row, London

Tel: +44 20 7734 5985

Henry Poole, while not the first tailor on the Row, certainly founded the reputation that it has to this day, and for that reason it is old-school royalty amongst the tailoring fraternity. It is the only firm to still be family-owned and family-run, with the line passing from Henry Poole to his cousin, Samuel Cundey, at the end of the nineteenth century and Angus Cundey still among the directors today. While Huntsman always had a reputation for being the most expensive shop on the Row (now no longer true), Henry Poole has always been quite modestly priced compared to its neighbours and yet loses nothing to reputation for tailoring excellence.

Norton & Sons

16 Savile Row, London

Tel: +44 20 7437 0829

Norton & Sons was revived a few years back by one Patrick Grant, a dashing business graduate who has succeeded in that short time in not only putting life back into a great tailoring name but also launching a ready-to-wear fashion line that is carried by department stores around the world (E. Tautz). Nortons was always most famous as a tailor of hunters and adventurers, and at one time created several new ways of keeping a British explorer dry, warm and elegant at the same time. Today the suits are of a structured shape with a firm shoulder; unique Scottish tweed is also a particular strength.

Jonathan Quearney

7 Windmill Street, London

Tel: +44 20 7631 5132

Jonathan is another example of a soft tailoring advocate, but tucked away from the rest up on

Windmill Street. He was trained by Thomas Mahon but has developed his own unique, contemporary shape and style. He is fascinated by craft but also has a peculiar gift for colour, always emphasising how customers have to be shown the coloured weaves in even the most basic-looking grey or blue suits.

Having set up his own shop six years ago, he has proved successful at communicating that soft approach to a new generation of bespoke customers. Recommended for those looking for a younger take on a classic cut.

Graham Browne

12 Well Court, London

Tel: +44 20 7248 7730

The only City tailor listed here (located in the business district of London), Graham Browne is a well-kept secret that I stumbled upon a few years ago. Recently rekindled by head cutter Russell Howarth, previously at military tailor Kashkets, this shop just off Bow Lane near to Bank station is possibly the best-value bespoke to be found anywhere in London. And unlike many tailors, Russell is always open to suggestion and experimentation – as evidenced by my odd requests and his work with Guy Hills of Dashing Tweeds.

New York

Americans love English tailoring, and for that reason as well as longevity and opportunism, Savile Row tailors dominate the business of bespoke suits in New York as well as in many other cities in the US. Most travel to the US twice a year and a good number make more than half their profits here. There are, however, still some great tailors based in New York – though those are mostly English or Italian and, a little like some of their visiting British peers, are getting on a bit.

Nino Corvato

510 Madison Ave, New York

Tel: +1 212 980 4980

Corvato has a very strong reputation among clients in the US and elsewhere. He favours a soft style, with almost imperceptible padding in the shoulder. Although originally from Sicily, he studied in Naples and moved to America in the 1960s. Prices start at around $3500. David Letterman is a famous client.

William Fioravanti

45 West 57th Street, New York

Tel: +1 212 355 1540

A Neapolitan tailor of the old school, Bill Fioravanti has lived in the US for a long time but has lost none of his love of the traditional tailoring techniques of his homeland. Something of a father figure to the industry in the US, he was President of the Custom Tailors Designers Association of America and back in the day won the Golden Scissors from the Academy of Master Tailors in Italy. The house fit is 'powerful', indicating a tendency to strong shoulders and suppressed waist.

Leonard Logsdail

9 East 53rd Street, 4th Floor, New York

Tel: +1 212 688 2868

Leonard Logsdail is an Englishman in New York. He originally trained on Savile Row, under Bernard Wetherill amongst others. (Wetherill was relaunched by Kilgour in 2010, as a separate bespoke house with a slightly different, hunting take on tailoring from the clean, modern aesthetics of Kilgour next door.) Today Len is based in midtown Manhattan, and has a charming little establishment shared with tailor and RTW-purveyor Stephen Kempton.

F Shattuck

Cazenovia, NY

Tel: +1 315 882 4724

Irish tailor Frank Shattuck is based in Cazenovia, in upstate New York, just outside Syracuse. He was on Madison Avenue for 10 years but moved out of the city a few years ago. Although not cheap, starting at $5800, this in part reflects the cost of construction in the US and the fact that Frank does all cutting and making himself. He also has a thing for polishing the buttons with olive oil.

Milan

Despite being the menswear fashion capital of the world, Milan does not excel on bespoke tailors. Great ready to wear, yes, and many of the best houses offer made to measure. But true bespoke is not that common. There are many claimants to the Caraceni name, all relatives but not all bespoke. Of the two bespoke houses, A Caraceni of Milan has the strongest reputation, though F Caraceni is also recommended. Ricciardi Giuseppe equally. Tindaro de Luca is a good tailor and enhanced his reputation by appearing on The Sartorialist as a well-dressed man about town.

F. Caraceni

Via San Marco 22, Milan

Tel: +39 02 6554284

Ferdinando Caraceni in Milan is probably the best-known of the bespoke houses that came out of the Caraceni family. With a spotless reputation, Caraceni is still seen as one of the best of all Italian tailors. Italian President Silvio Berlusconi was the house's most famous client, until he switched to Kiton in 2010 to the consternation of tailoring obsessives everywhere.

Tindaro de Luca

Via Gesu 15, Milan

Tel: +39 02 7602109

Tindaro is based on the chic Via Gesu, bang in the middle of the Golden Triangle of Milanese fashion and next to the Kiton showroom. He has none of the strut or show of his close neighbours, but makes a well-regarded bespoke suit with a relatively strong chest for Italy but soft shoulder – certainly not along the lines of the classic Milanese business suit. Tindaro achieved a certain prominence after being photographed by Scott Schuman of The Sartorialist, wearing a fine chalk stripe suit with a buff waistcoat.

Hong Kong

Hong Kong is the exact opposite of Milan – lots and lots of tailors, but very few of them are any good. Walk down streets in parts of Kowloon and you will be assailed by people offering to make you a suit. In how many places in the world does that happen? Unfortunately, many of them will offer to make you 'bespoke' in 24 hours. Which obviously means it isn't bespoke. As you will never see where these suits are made, reputation is key to knowing whether you are getting value for money in the construction.

For the cheapest end of bespoke tailors in London, you can get a very nice suit in Hong Kong (around £800 and up). In this high end of the market the tailors with the best reputation are W.W. Chan, H. Baroman and A. Man Hing Cheong. For the mid-range (more like £400), Edward Tam of E. Italian is very good value.

A-Man Hing Cheong

5 Connaught Rd, Mandarian Oriental Hotel,
Hong Kong

Tel: +852 2522 3336

The atmosphere at A-Man is friendly, clubby and collegiate. The dark wood interior puts customers at their ease and regular clients frequently pop by to run through fittings or flick through cloth books. Most Hong Kong tailors don't have much of a house style, but you could certainly make an argument that A-Man does – a fairly classic English shape, with some structure to the chest and shoulders. It also tends to favour English cloths. Compared to its close cousins below, A-Man also tends to use fewer details like horn buttons.

H. Baroman

9 Queen's Road, Central Hong Kong

Tel: +852 2523 3238

W.W. Chan

A2, 2/F, Burlington House, 94 Nathan Road,
Kowloon, Hong Kong

Tel: +852 2366 9738

Both W.W. Chan and H. Baroman are old Shanghai tailors, established in that city early in the twentieth century and only relatively recently having arrived in Hong Kong. Known back then as the red gang, these tailors set up an apprentice scheme that trained many of today's master tailors. Along with A-Man Hing Cheong, these two in particular have become firm favourites with visiting sartorialists from the US and UK. Not cheap by any means, but approaching Savile Row standards for a considerable discount.

E. Italian

Shop 117, 1/F, Regal Kowloon Hotel,
71 Mody Road, Kowloon, Hong Kong

Tel: +852 23672782

Though hard to distinguish immediately from any of the three or four tailors also based in the Regal Kowloon, Edward Tam's establishment E. Italian deserves individual recognition for the dedication of the service and quality of the workmanship at a very reasonable price – between £300 and £400. This is budget bespoke without any of the fakery of Hong Kong's many overnight tailors. Edward will refuse to make a suit without a basted fitting. Although certainly not of the quality of the larger establishments above, this is worth a look for those on a budget.

France

Paris might not be the centre of menswear today, but back in the 1950s it was where every tailor wanted to make his reputation.

Camps de Luca

11 Place de la Madeleine, Paris

Tel: +33 142 65 42 15

One of Paris's two great tailoring establishments. After forging a reputation in Milan, Mario de Luca teamed up with Joseph Camps, who was revered across Paris for his originality and invention. He was the showman to Mario's diligent, management character. Today the shop is run by Mario's son and grandson, Marc and Charles de Luca. The house has a reputation for a sharp silhouette and little innovations like a tear-shaped inside pocket.

Cifonelli

33 Rue Marbeuf, Paris

Tel: +33 143 59 39 13

Cousins Massimo and Lorenzo Cifonelli now run this establishment, having started in the workshop in 1993 and taken over in 2003. They say the house style combines the best of English, French and Italian tailoring: flair, strong structure and precise detailing. Cifonelli now also offers MTM and RTW. The jackets all feature the typical strong and forward shoulder, as well as some great details like exterior pockets on the sleeve and curved patch pockets

» Finishing touches

Linings

Once you've selected the cloth for your suit (material, colour and pattern) as well as the style (number of buttons and breasts) there's just the annoying details that you've probably given zero thought to in advance. This includes pockets, linings and buttons.

Bright colours

Don't be afraid to get a bright lining if you are not driven by a transitory trend. Bright red has long been a classic accompaniment to navy, for example, from socks to scarves. So a red lining in a navy suit is not necessarily trendy.

Classic colours

However, if you want colour, it's generally better to stick to dark but unusual tones – rich, deep shades of purple, green, blue and burnt orange. Think of the choice in the same way you think about your tie. The tie colours that really draw admiration are not flashy yellows but purple with navy, orange with brown, a green with mid-grey flannel.

As your lining is made of the same material as your tie (well, a similar one, silk is rarely used today as it doesn't breathe well and manmade fibres last better) and contrasts with the suit cloth in the same way, the process of colour selection should be the same. Except that you can't change your lining. So think about it like this – if you could only ever wear one tie with that suit, what colour would it be?

Colour combinations

Other colour combinations I recommend are gold or copper with grey, bottle green with blue and purple with charcoal. With tweeds, bright colours often work very well, probably because most will have some bright colours woven in there, in however small a quantity.

Match to the jacket

If you want to be safe, though, go with a lining that is similar to the suit. Like your socks rather than your tie – same colour, perhaps a touch darker. This is

Copies and fads

Over the past 10 years flashy linings have become much more common. Scarlets, yellows and bright stripes, all intended to give a touch of individuality to a suit.

Paul Smith was a genuine innovator here as he was in much else. But as everyone copied him, bright linings became ordinary, even cheap. Soon everyone on the high street was doing it, by which time the trend was dead.

A similar thing happened with buttonholes, working buttons on the cuffs and high fastenings. All trends, all ephemeral, and when the dust settled Savile Row was still doing what it has always done, and doing it very well.

the lining that no one will notice, and is definitely recommended if your suit is otherwise quite striking. A bold check, for instance, or contrast buttons. It's all a question of balance.

Lining patterns

Follow a similar philosophy for lining patterns: only be as bold as the suit will allow. Beware, though – if anything a bold pattern can appear cheaper than a bold colour. Avoid polka dots and paisley designs unless very subtle.

Other lining options include football strips – famously incorporated into suit jackets by Pogson & Davis of Mayfair. Or indeed shirtings – although not as slippery as silk-like materials, they work well enough in a half-lined jacket or just to tape the seams of unlined jackets. The thin strip used as tape means a bold pattern can become a subtle suggestion.

Words from the wise

Michael Drake, Founder,
Drake's, UK

» Style is all about the details

It doesn't matter how beautifully your suit has been cut (or what it cost), you will not be well dressed without paying attention to some rather simple details. Key among those is the tie.

The best ties are handmade, never stitched by machine. Avoid extremes, no wider than nine centimetres and no narrower than seven. The pattern should not be overly designed, with too many colours, or too shiny. The tradition of lighter coloured ties in the morning, a little darker in the afternoon and darker still in the evening is hard to beat.

There are only two knots worth considering: the four in hand and the half Windsor, the second also being a good standby if the tie is too long or a slightly fuller knot is required.

In an ideal world the tie should reach the top of the trouser waistband with both the front and tail finishing at the same length. If this can't be achieved, better to have the tail slightly longer than the front.

Choosing your buttons

Your choice of buttons will have an impact on your suit, and there's plenty to consider when it comes to options: number of buttons, material, colour. Buttons can be fun to shop for and there are some great online sources. Few, however, will stock matching sets in the sizes required for the front and cuffs. Make sure they do before you explore too readily. Buttons should always match.

Material

The buttons of most good suits are made with horn, made from the actual horn of animals such as cow, deer or buffalo. They're tougher and tend to have nicer, richer colour tones than plastic.

Having said that, they make little overall difference to a suit and if there were one thing you could sacrifice in a jacket it would probably be horn.

Handsewn button holes

The best bespoke suit will be entirely made by hand, and that should also include the buttonholes. You will be able to tell the difference as a handsewn buttonhole will have bulkier stitches and they may be a tiny bit irregular. On the inside, the stitching will be visibly rougher.

(Followed by handmade shoulder pads and some hand sewing. At the other end of the scale would be bespoke fittings – never give them up.)

Blazer buttons can be experimented with quite freely, with gilt versions the most classic. Avoid a crest unless it is yours or your club's, school's or college's. Personally I dislike the associations with gilt-buttoned blazers and prefer alternative high-contrast colours like white, cream or silver. Covered buttons, where the cloth of the jacket or lapels covers the button entirely, are most common on dinner jackets.

Other great natural materials to shop for are shell and wood. Mother-of-pearl buttons are standard on good shirts, but they can also look well on pale jackets, and black versions equally on high-shine

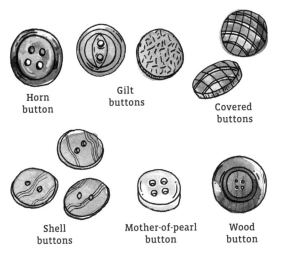

Horn button

Gilt buttons

Covered buttons

Shell buttons

Mother-of-pearl button

Wood button

materials such as mohair or silk. Wooden buttons give heft and texture (rather like leather, another option when braided for odd jackets). In general if opting for unusual materials, it is advisable to go for a slightly darker tone than you would otherwise.

Colour

Generally buttons will match the cloth they go with. So a navy suit will have dark-blue buttons, a grey suit dark-grey ones. Like a matching suit lining, they tend to be similar but ever so slightly darker. Paler buttons can't help but look cheap.

However, there isn't that much variety to be had with grey or blue. By far the nicest horn buttons are in brown. From darkest chocolate to palest chestnut, brown horn buttons will contain more variations in tone and swirls of pattern.

And if you usually wear brown shoes with your suits rather than black (as I do) I highly recommend brown buttons. If black shoes are the norm, best to stick with matching buttons.

With odd jackets, which will of their nature most often be worn with brown shoes, brown horn buttons work very well. Particularly as there will also likely be pattern and texture in the jacket to play against.

Holes

Most buttons have four holes, the better to be secured and be symmetrical. But some will have two, which is a design quirk that some men like, particularly on dark-blue buttons. Nothing wrong with that – and if they are sewn on by hand they're unlikely to come off any time soon.

Buttons on cuffs

Cuffs can have one, two, three, four or five buttons – even none if that's the look desired. Four is standard, and I would avoid three. Five is for when extra decoration is desired, while two is old fashioned and one fashion-forward. Turn-back cuffs will generally have two buttons or none at all.

Associations with working cuffs

Working buttonholes used to be a sign of bespoke clothing. The buttons on your cuffs would actually undo all the way up, allowing you to wash your hands without getting the cuff wet. Ready-to-wear jackets hadn't done it for years, so those that did had to be bespoke. Men would undo the first of these buttons as a subtle indication of bespoke.

Then about 10 years ago, ready to wear started including working buttonholes alongside other design details like coloured stitching and hand-stitched lapels. Suddenly these things weren't a sign of bespoke, quite the opposite.

Interestingly, Anderson & Sheppard traditionally made its suits without working cuffs. So to them it was never a sign of bespoke.

The standard pockets

Pockets – so easy to appear so dull. Not many options, you'd think. But a suit can come alive with the pockets.

Standard options

If you want a standard suit, and the tailor asks you what pockets you require, tell him: two outer hip pockets, straight and flapped; one plain outer breast pocket; two inner breast pockets; and probably one internal ticket pocket. This last is the small pocket on the inside left of the jacket that was probably used originally for tickets; today it is sometimes used for change but, most often, contains business cards. Such are the evolving needs of society.

Normal hip pockets are bags sewn into the inside of a jacket. If you have an unlined jacket you can see them hanging there, often tacked to the inside so they don't snag. The outer opening, a slit, is covered by a

Standard pockets   **Welted pockets**   **Patch pockets**

flap. This is largely to make its appearance cleaner, as otherwise the slit can sag and look unattractive.

Welt pockets

However, a pocket without a flap (called a besom or welt pocket) is common on dressier outfits such as a dinner jacket. It used to be common on normal suits in the twenties and thirties as well, but then suits were made of such thick stuff that a flap added greater proportionate bulk.

Today welt pockets can remain as clean, crisp slits if they are rarely used to contain anything – a slip of paper at the most. Many tailors would recommend keeping them basted up to make sure they never sag. Indeed, some men do this with all their pockets, flapped or welt. It dissuades them from ever putting anything in there (see page 133). A good alternative is to have smaller sections sewn into the inside of the hip pocket, perhaps split into two across the pocket's width.

The outer breast pocket is not flapped, but has an extra strip of cloth sewn across its front instead. This

Slanted pockets   **Curved pockets**   **Slanted welt pockets**

is the pocket your handkerchief should go in –
arranged in a casual, degagé air; in fact just stuff it in
there. Some patch pockets have a similar design,
with a strip across the top to give them bulk.

Patch pockets

Patch pockets are a simpler design, created by
sewing a patch of material onto the outside of the
jacket rather than a bag onto the inside. If welts are
more dressy, patches are more casual. They are most
often found on the more casual type of jacket –
summer, tweed, hacking, and other types of odd.

On a suit jacket they are an easy way to make it
appear more casual and, perhaps, make it suitable for
wearing separately. The cloth must be casual (thick
or rough). Another thing that helps that impression is
the addition of an external ticket pocket. This is most
usually positioned above the right hip pocket
(presuming the wearer to be right handed) and is
narrow but deep, in order to suit a vertically slotted
ticket. Appropriate on any style of suit really, but
definitely a casual design element.

Experimenting with shape

All our pockets so far have been straight. They can
also be slanted or even curved. Slanted pockets were
originally conceived to make access easy on
horseback. As a result they are common on hacking
jackets today. On suits, however, they are seen as
dressier than straight pockets, as the diagonals create
a sharper look. Curved pockets are a lovely
eccentricity, but should be reserved for tweeds and
gun club jackets.

Additions to the suit

While this book is definitively about suits and not the things that are worn with them, it is worth saying a few words on the various connections.

Shirts

As with black tie, the style and formality of a shirt is worth considering in relation to the suit it is being worn with. It looks rather odd to sport a knockabout corduroy suit with a white, spread collar and double-cuffed shirt. Go for a tattersall or an Oxford cloth instead, and single cuffs.

The fit of a shirt should also parallel that of the suit in a few ways. There's little point having a trim jacket if the shirt underneath billows at the waist – the effect is rather undermined when you take the jacket off. And a jacket with a high armhole should be worn with a similarly tight-holed shirt to take full advantage of the extra movement this design allows.

Ties

Ties are really a question of style rather than fit. From printed foulards through various wovens into square-ended knitted ties, there is a formality scale that should be mimicked in the suit. But one thing that is worth bearing in mind with the 'fit' of a tie is that the front blade should finish on the waistband of the trousers; the rear blade should be the same length or, if that's impossible, a little longer. Some very sartorial gentlemen even tuck that rear blade into their trousers. Whatever your height or personal

» In the fold

Different ways of counting folds have become
confused, and today any multi-fold tie (more than
three folds) is often called a seven-fold tie.

Most normal ties have three obvious folds. If you
look at the back of the front blade, the silk has been
folded in on itself on either side, and one of those
flaps has just been tucked under creating a small,
third fold. While retaining the same width of those
two sides, the silk can be folded in on itself almost as
many times as you like. You just have to start with
more silk, and the tie becomes thicker. The folds go
right through the tie (or do on a good one) and can
be seen on the back blade, though this might be hard
to see as the first folds will be quite high up inside.

You can spot a real seven-fold because for a tie to
have an uneven number it must either have a little
lip like the three-folds or the folds must overlap and
concertina into each other.

style, the length of your tie is obviously related to where you wear your trousers and is therefore worth considering in bespoke.

Handkerchiefs

Finally handkerchiefs, my favourite accessory. The outer breast pocket always looks rather naked – or pointless – without something in it so I recommend at least a white linen square. Silks are for wearing with rougher cloths or when one is not sporting a tie. Too much silk otherwise. The only element of wearing a handkerchief that is relevant to a suit is that a lower buttoning position on the jacket will mean its lapel overlaps the pocket slightly. I like this – the handkerchief should peep. If the buttoning is higher, the pocket and thus its handkerchief can be rather isolated. If you decide you like that effect, worth bearing it in mind when you design your first bespoke suit.

Directory of suppliers

There are many fine shirtmaking houses around the world – indeed many bespoke tailors will measure you up for a great bespoke shirt as well, though of course the shirts will unlikely be made in-house, unlike the suits. Of these many options, two names are by far and away the most famous and with good reason. One is French and the other English – Charvet and Turnbull & Asser.

Charvet

28 Place Vendome, Paris

As a silk trader and former visiting shirtmaker, Charvet knows its cloths and manufacturing details. The headquarters in Paris is a must-visit and as well as the shirts I highly recommend their ties, which knot especially well despite their standard construction. Also carried in many department stores, such as Bergdorf Goodman and Selfridge's.

Turnbull & Asser

71 & 72 Jermyn Street, London, SW1Y 6PF

Le Snob ESSENTIAL T&A is now one of the very last vestiges of great shirtmaking on Jermyn Street. With its own factory in Gloucester, and its own exclusive cloths, this is shirtmaking as it used to be. The reputation is for relatively stiff shirts with floating collars but reinforced points and plackets. And the reputation for rather adventurous colour is also well deserved. But that doesn't mean Turnbull

& Asser can't make you a wonderfully soft Oxford button-down shirt, in plain unadventurous blue. And all measured on site, transferred to paper patterns and shipped off to Gloucester. T&A is also a general purveyor of everything from suits to sweaters, in the Jermyn Street mould; but I'd prioritise the shirts above all else. T&A also have branches in New York and Beverly Hills.

Lock & Co

6 St James's Street, London, SW1A 1EF

Founded in 1676 to serve the court of Charles II down the road at St James's, Lock & Co is a wonderfully storied, modest British institution. Nothing seems to have changed in all those years. The distinctive white hat boxes are still stacked around the walls, the staff as polite and deferential as ever and, most importantly, the quality of the headgear is still the finest you will find. I particularly recommend the travelling fedora, complete with delightful tube version of the hat box to roll it up in.

Drake's

www.drakes-london.com

Although only available from the company online, it is stocked wholesale in many department stores. A relative newcomer to the world of retail, Drake's has for a few years been making ties for the biggest names around the world – all by hand, all at the company's workshop in London. Since launching itself online, both ties and scarves (the company's starting point) have been very popular. Key to the success has been the colour sense of founder

Michael Drake, in recent seasons exhibiting itself for example in sugary colours inspired by the British raj. Linen has been particularly well used as a material in both products.

Dunhill

2 Davies Street, London, W1K 3DJ

Although the leather luggage-maker has become somewhat more over the years, with its own series of 'houses' now around the world, I particularly recommend Dunhill for its accessories. Silk handkerchiefs are tasteful and well made, silver cufflinks are a standby and the leather goods are worthy of any man's investment. Look out for the Alfred Dunhill collection, made by hand at a factory in north London – where the company's famous pipes are also hand-wrought. Other branches in almost 50 other countries worldwide.

Albert Thurston

www.albertthurston.com

The best maker of braces, or suspenders, anywhere in the world. Not many men today where braces, but for those that do I can't recommend anywhere more highly than Albert Thurston. Stored by tailors everywhere, but also available on the company's website. Worth trying on first, however, to make sure you get the right length. The most popular style involves the excess hanging down in front of the waistband, and you don't want that too long.

Tom Ford

(For details see page 57)

As with suits, shirts and much else, the quality of Tom Ford's merchandise is impressive and I would recommend the accessories as highly as the ready to wear. As you would probably expect, the patterns are often bold but the colour schemes often subtle enough to push the accessory into the background. For those that like a thick blade and a long knot, the ties will be the best you can find.

Kiton

(For details see page 56)

Always worth visiting for shirts and accessories. The shirts, you will notice, are hemmed by hand, creating a seam along the bottom that most resembles a well-rolled handkerchief. Also known for little innovations like ties made out of a single piece of exclusive worsted suit cloth.

Rubinacci

(For details see page 59)

Le Snob ESSENTIAL Accessories aplenty here in surprising colours and combinations. Silk scarves and handkerchiefs featuring scenes of naples; scarves flamboyant in Aztec-like designs; umbrellas made by Brigg but personalised for Rubinacci with bright colours and polished knobs of wood. Seven-fold ties with the lightest of linings too, as well as the knit ties in unusual colours as popularised by the son of the current owner, Luca Rubinacci.

» Occasionwear

Rules for black tie

A man's dress used to be driven by social propriety – what his peers considered to be fit and proper. Most of the rules for dress that we have inherited were formalised by social norms. Style icons were made when those that could broke with convention and wore new combinations, such as Edward VIII wearing suede shoes and double-breasted jackets. He made that acceptable – but he was not necessarily the first to do so, just the first to sufficiently encourage others to follow his lead.

Today, there is little of this social propriety left. Men in some offices know they have to wear a suit and smart shoes. Some social fixtures, such as race meetings, have dress codes. But that's about it. Today the only area where men know their dress is prescribed is when wearing a dinner jacket, or black tie.

Cover the waist

However, common mistakes are still made with black tie. The biggest is that a man's waist is often not covered. With black tie you have three options: waistcoat, cummerbund or double-breasted jacket. All cover the waist and conceal that part of the shirt. They are listed in declining order of formality (unlike most other areas of dress, double-breasted is considered less formal than single) and a man must wear one of them.

This choice then goes some way to determining the shirt a man wears. Most evening shirts have stiff or starched fronts in some shape. A small or oval front is designed to sit under a waistcoat, so only that part of the shirt is exposed when one's jacket is open. A cummerbund leaves more of the shirt exposed and must therefore be worn with a wider stiff front in a rectangular shape. Being less formal, it may also be worn with a pleated front and turned-down collar. Stiff-fronted shirts most often have a wing collar, though this is not universal.

« **Cover the waist** From far left, waistcoat, cummerbund, and double-breasted jacket.

Other common errors

So the second biggest mistake men make is to mis-match the formality of waist covering, shirt front and collar. Each is on a sliding scale and must not be too far apart from the others.

The third biggest mistake men make is wearing black tie during the day, something the Americans are particularly guilty of. Black tie is evening wear.

The jacket should have a peaked collar, rather than a notch or step. This reflects the outfit's antecedents in the morning and frock coats. A shawl collar is acceptable but is more casual. It is often found on double-breasted or smoking jackets – or indeed more casual dinner jackets like a tropical-weight ecru, famously worn by Humphrey Bogart in *Casablanca*.

Colour variations in black tie

While black tie is generally black, as you might expect, it can in fact be midnight blue, brown or any other dark colour. Noel Coward had a brown outfit, complete with matching tie and pumps, made for him by Douglas Howard. Some rakes of the past have worn dinner jackets in all the colours you commonly see smoking jackets in today. However, generally only the first of these alternatives – midnight blue – is recommended.

A touch of individuality

There are areas of the black tie ensemble where you can add a touch of your own individuality – know the rules, then twist them: that's the motto here.

Shoes

Shoes for black tie should be, at the least, highly polished black Oxfords. The Oxford is cleaner than the Derby, and so more formal. Brogueing is also informal, so shouldn't be worn with black tie. While black Oxfords are fine, patent is better for being that bit shinier. The whole of the black tie ensemble is about contrasting textures – wool of suit with silk of lapels, seam on trousers or shine of bow tie. Patent enhances that contrast. And although many men don't like the artificial finish, a delicate patent shoe with a thin, cemented sole is really much smarter.

Formal white

Counter-intuitive though it may be, there is nothing wrong with wearing a white bow tie with black tie. The adjective does not refer to the colour of the bow tie but to the overall dominant colour of the outfit.

However, a man today is likely to be castigated by the ignorant for wearing a white bow tie. So instead, try wearing a white waistcoat in the same stiff Marcella material as your dress shirt, instead of a black one that would echo the jacket. Again, a white waistcoat is not wrong, merely more formal. And a white waistcoat will ultimately stand out far less than a white bow tie.

Most white waistcoats will be backless, with merely a collar and elastic at the waist. Both white and black can be made as such, and it is far more comfortable; the device was probably invented originally by shirtmakers Hawes & Curtis.

Keep the jacket on

Of course, it goes without saying that you would never take your dinner jacket off, so the back of the shirt would never be revealed under the waistcoat. Indeed, black tie is the outfit that demonstrates this maxim of menswear better than any other. Every item, from the waistcoat to the shirt to the cummerbund, would lose its elegance if the jacket were removed.

There used to be a tradition of patterning the non-display parts of one's shirt with humorous motifs, like animals or cartoon characters, merely to demonstrate this point. But that goes down as needlessly loud personality, hidden or not – why would a man ever want his black tie attire to be humorous?

The little extras

Black tie is so simple, the little extras can be important for the outfit. Start with a nice white handkerchief.

Handkerchiefs

Most of the time linen would be recommended for a white handkerchief: it is clean, crisp and the slight roughness of the cloth is a nice contrast to the silk of a neck tie. But that's for daywear. At night, it is natural for the handkerchief to reflect the lustre of the bow tie, lapels and trouser seams, rather than contrast with them, so choose silk, worn in a puff. The easiest way to achieve this is to take one corner of the handkerchief and stuff it into your pocket until it reaches the bottom. Then take the opposite corner and stuff it behind the first one, carrying on stuffing the body in until only a couple of inches of puff are on display. The fact that one corner is touching the bottom will prevent the handkerchief slipping down.

As for linen, there is certainly licence here to be more decorative than during the day so fold it into a three or four-point arrangement: fold each corner up until it is beside the top one, clustering the four together. Then fold in the sides and stuff it.

You could have a little colour here. Certainly have it in the handkerchief rather than the bow tie or cummerbund. Good colours for a silk pocket handkerchief could be scarlet, purple or gold. Anything that looks rich and luxurious, preferably with some delicate pattern.

Boutonniere

The other option is to have colour only in your boutonniere. The flowers, often carnations, lilies or roses, should be neat and secured with a loop of thread behind the lapel. Red is best, but also yellow or white. Perhaps a deep red clove carnation or a hybrid tea rose in white.

Bow ties

The bow tie should, obviously, be one that you tie yourself. If you wear a wing collar, it should also be sized to your neck so that no join is visible at the back. Get a size bigger than the shirt you would normally wear, as it can always be made smaller by tying a little more loosely.

Generally though, the aim is to tie the bow tie securely but not too neatly. It should be obvious that it is not pre-tied – not because you want to show off, but because a little *sprezzatura* is always more elegant.

Finishing touches

There are many other finishing touches you can apply to black tie, but they should always be of secondary importance. Pocket watches in the waistcoat are nice, though nicest with a fob in the middle. A smart topcoat in black – perhaps with a velvet collar or at least peak lapels – is also a pleasant addition. A silk scarf or cane seems rather excessive. The last three are harder to justify given that no one at the event will see you wearing them. Unless you stroll around inside in your outerwear, rather than checking it at the door. And this is the last area of propriety, remember.

Occasionwear suppliers

Favourbrook

Menswear: 55 Jermyn Street, London
Accessories: 19–21 Piccadilly Arcade

Although a relative newcomer among its neighbours on Jermyn Street, and the tailors on Savile Row, Favourbrook is the only establishment in London where one can find excellently tailored occasionwear from the classic to the frankly frivolous. From fancy waistcoats to made-to-measure morning suits, Favourbrook is a great resource for inspiration – I recommend a quick trip for ideas in the run-up to any big event. For greater discretion, experiment with pale colours and subtle detailing, such as a sugary pink waistcoat with lace embroidery.

Budd

1–3 Piccadilly Arcade, London, SW1Y 6NH

 A mere matter of metres away from Favourbrook's waistcoat selection is Budd – a traditional shirtmaker through and through. It doesn't do email; it doesn't do slim cuts. But it makes some of the best bespoke dress shirts to be found anywhere in the world. Classic stiff, detachable, wing collars are not easy to find today: so many are poor, short, flimsy imitations. Budd will have the right thing, together with some great accessories. Ask to see the bespoke shirtmaking upstairs if you get a chance.

Peckham Rye

11 Newburgh Street, London, W1F 7RW

It's an old rhyming slang phrase for 'tie'. And it's a small and relatively modern-looking establishment best known in the UK for its skinny neck ties. But for occasionwear look past the ties towards the silk scarves, which are amongst the very few in the UK to still be made – most importantly, fringed – by hand. For the evening they have white silk ties, both plain and spun to feel like cashmere. I particularly like those faced with both types of silk, one on each side, to hang casually around the neck on the way to an event.

James Smith & Sons

53 New Oxford Street, London WC1A 1BL

Many storied establishments will sell you a great walking stick to accompany white tie. Swaine Adeney & Brigg would be another recommendation. But little compares to the experience of going into James Smith & Sons, that slightly ragged, rather dusty establishment at the end of the Tottenham Court Road. Lack of frills means value for money. And with a little pressing, great service to make sure your exacting needs are met. I highly recommend them for umbrellas.

Charvet

(For details see page 113)

As listed elsewhere, an excellent source of all shirting and accessories, for occasion as much as business wear. Dress shirts, bow ties, silk scarves: I recommend describing your desires to the sales staff and letting them guide you. Worth the trip to Paris on its own. From London, anyway.

Brioni

(For details see page 56)

Brioni had long dressed James Bond as played by various actors, until Tom Ford took on that responsibility for Daniel Craig. That is just one of

UNIQUE » RARE » LITTLE-KNOWN » ULTIMATE Snob

Pumps and slippers The ultimate footwear for black tie is black pumps with a silk bow. These look like open-topped shoes, a little like ballet pumps. But they have a bow across the top that, like one's bow tie, should match the lapels of the jacket (usually grosgrain silk, rather than satin). Unsurprisingly, many men don't like pumps. But with the most formal versions of black tie, they are correct.

Velvet slippers, at first glance, could appear to be similar. But they're actually at the other end of the formality scale. Created to be worn around the home, they are a casual option and best paired with informal black tie such as a velvet smoking jacket, which again was often worn for entertaining at home (once general formality had slid to the point that a dinner jacket was standard outside the home). Velvet is a soft, homey material – wear the slippers and the jacket together.

the reasons that men associate Brioni with great evening wear, the others being its reputation for incredibly elegant yet lightweight suits. Luxury, with Italian style.

Tom Ford

(For details see page 57)

Tom Ford has sold his brand on sex appeal and it is therefore no surprise that the dinner jacket, with its suggestion of meetings in the night, cuts a special dash when styled by Mr Ford. Expect sweeping lapels, a nipped waist and the closest thing you will get to an Atlas silhouette. Cloths, too, are a source of brash experimentation for those that want it. There are bow ties (large), cummerbunds and velvet slippers (high-heeled, high-waisted) to match.

Henry Poole

15 Savile Row, London, W1S 3PJ

Anyone on or around Savile Row will cut you an excellent black or white tie. I would simply recommend that you go to whoever you have the greatest experience with and faith in. The only reason I pick out Henry Poole here is that I have personal experience of their velvet jackets. But fit and therefore the expertise of your own tailor is paramount.

» Possess

Suit maintenance

The most important things for suit maintenance are nothing to do with cleaning or pressing, but what you do with the suit when you take it off. Whether cleaning or storing a suit, or just hanging it up in your wardrobe, you need to take care to retain the shape and avoid damaging the fabric.

A bespoke suit has a very specific three-dimensional shape that has been designed to fit your body. When it is not hanging on that body, and moulding its chest to yours, it needs to be draped around something that is similar in shape. This is most important for the shoulders, because their dominant line is horizontal while the rest of the suit is vertical. They suffer the most when a suit is just dropped on the floor.

Hanging up a suit

So the first thing you need is a hanger with decent shoulders to it. This means that the two ends of the hanger must be as wide as possible. It is good if the breadth of the hanger from end to end is similar to your own; never use a women's hanger for a men's jacket or vice versa. Equally, it is nice if the hanger can be in a natural wood, so it absorbs and deodorises any moisture accumulated during wear.

However, neither of these things is as important as just hanging up your suit every day. Get home, take off your jacket; lay it on the bed, fold the trousers and hang them carefully; then repeat with the jacket. Make sure that the suit has a little breathing room in the wardrobe, to avoid creating new creases. Don't hang it on the back of a chair, whatever shape. That is most likely to distort. If you don't have a hanger, fold the jacket carefully in half and lay over the bed or chair.

If hung well, trousers should retain their crease for quite a while. When it needs firming up, either use a trouser press or an iron – just make sure to set the latter on a low heat and put a tea towel on top of the cloth. Direct heat will create a shininess to the wool.

Packing a suit for travel

When you're travelling with a suit, it helps if you have a suitcase that is as long as your jacket. To pack, turn the jacket inside-out, making sure to pull through the shoulders. Fold the collar up and, holding the jacket by the reversed shoulders, fold it in half. Lay it in the suitcase and make sure it is packed securely all around. Because the inside of the jacket is facing outwards, there is less risk of nicking or otherwise damaging the wool.

If you don't have a suitcase that large, fold the jacket again lengthways, at a point just below the waist button. This should mean you are not folding the external pockets, which are hard to fold neatly. Trousers are simple to fold, though again it helps a lot if you have a suitcase that is as wide as half the trousers' waist. If you don't, fold the trousers into thirds and place in the centre of the case.

Cleaning and care

As with shoes, it helps the long-term upkeep of your suit immensely if you brush it down at the end of every day. A soft clothes brush, briefly passed over the jacket and trousers, will remove surface dirt and dust that is all around us during the day and gets into the fibres, wearing them down.

It's good to do this every day, but not essential. You might not always be bothered to do so, after a night out, for example, though that's still no excuse to leave the jacket on the floor either. Just try and brush as much as you can – far better to do it irregularly than not at all.

Dry cleaning

Everyone dry cleans their suits too often. If you could see how dry cleaning is done, you would avoid it like the plague. The suit is spun around in a vast drum, mixing with chemicals, and then pressed in an equally large machine that squashes the whole thing flat. Not good for the three-dimensional chest or shoulders, as mentioned previously. In fact, it can ruin the good work your tailor has done to make the jacket fit. What's more, the chemicals don't so much get rid of the dirt as dilute it and spread it around.

When you do get the suit dry cleaned, use a professional. Who counts as a professional? Well, I would say someone that also steams and presses a suit – which is what you should be doing in between dry cleaning.

Words from the wise

Stephen Haughton Owner,
Burford Valet Service, UK

» Keep your pockets free

Many years ago, after my weekly visit to the
Connaught Hotel to return a couple of suits to Alec
Guinness (made for him by the late, great Dougie
Hayward), I was walking back to my little van with a
smile on my face. Mr Guinness, that quintessential
English gentleman, had given me some advice that
I've never forgotten.

"Mr Guinness, your suits are such a pleasure to
press, so shapely and balanced," I had observed.
"Dear boy," he replied, "the secret is that I never
carry bulky items in my pockets; just a slim pen, a
notepad, a handkerchief or two of course, and a bill
fold. If I do have change it goes into my ticket
pocket. Everything else is in the holdall. The suit
stays crisp and it means I hardly ever put my hands
in the pockets, so there's no build up of grime."

I've practiced that religiously ever since.

How much to dry clean?

There is some disagreement about how often you should dry clean a suit. Everything from once a month to absolutely never. Despite being aware of the dangers of dry cleaning, some men declare it necessary because men are just messy, particularly in the bathroom. An occasional sprinkle is inevitable. Others retain never dry cleaning as a point of absolute principle. Those men tend to be older and, in my experience, are unlikely to sponge and press their suits much either.

Realistically, it depends on how you wear the suit and how often. The range should be between every six months and every five years, depending on those factors. If you wear the suit once a week to work, perhaps keep the trousers on when you get home, and never go out clubbing in it, then being dry cleaned once a year should be fine.

Seasonal clean

Many men have everything dry cleaned before they put it away for the season – packing away their summer linen and getting out the winter flannel. That's certainly the right way round to do it: never pack things away dirty.

Steam and press

A steam and press involves a gentleman (historically, one's valet) pushing steam through the cloth in much the same way that an iron does, though not as fierce or as close, and then using an iron to smooth the cloth back to perfection. He will use various curved blocks to do this on, so that the chest, shoulders and sleeve retain their impeccable three-dimensional shape.

If you dry clean your suits once a year, have them steamed and pressed once every three months (assuming the kind of wear described opposite). It is particularly nice to do when you return from travelling, as all packing will create some creases. Most good hotels will also provide this service for you when you arrive at your destination.

Recommendations

One good tip I was given for finding a steam-and-press man was to find the Four Seasons hotel in a particular city and ask them where they send their dry cleaning. I've tried this twice in large cities, and it has worked. Always best to have a personal recommendation.

Seasonal storage

When one gets to the luxurious stage of having too many suits to comfortably hang in a wardrobe, it's worth thinking about ways to effectively store them over the Spring/Summer season, and then over Autumn/Winter. This doesn't necessarily mean having two exact sets of clothes – there can be overlaps, most suits are at least two-season. But it makes sense to put away overcoats, gloves and heavy sweaters during the summer, as well as the heavier tweed and flannel suits. Equally, summer cloths like linen and cotton could effectively be put away for the winter.

Store all items clean, so any dirt is not worked into the cloth and doesn't attract mould or infestation. Fold carefully and separate with tissue paper if you have any. I tend to store in my suitcases, but if you can do so in another environment that is clean and dry that is preferable (and easier). Then have everything pressed by a professional when it comes out. And if you get to the stage of storing shoes as well as clothes, you've really made it.

» Discover

Share and discover

As with so many of the world's niche obsessions today, there are several style forums and blogs where you can find out more than you ever wanted to know about bespoke tailoring. There are personal experiences, geeky arguments and pages and pages of 'shoe porn' – where fans post pictures of their favourite shoes, from revealing angles.

As a reference tool, they are invaluable. If you need first-hand reports on tailors or brands, just type it into the search function and you'll find a myriad of ratings and rantings. Equally valuable is information on little known styles, tailoring quirks or points of historical interest.

Among the Internet resources, there are three major forums: 'Style Forum', 'Ask Andy About Clothes' and the 'London Lounge'. Although the first two are theoretically American and the third European, in practice contributors come from all over the world and are often participants in more than one. AAAC was founded by Andy Gilchrist, who offers his own guide to clothes, available on CD, and the 'London Lounge' by Michael Alden. Michael also has the best video blog out there on men's style, 'Dress With Style'.

As to other blogs, the biggest out there is 'A Suitable Wardrobe', run by Will Boelhke out of San Francisco. Will is an artful illustrator of the strengths of classic style, with a particular touch for colour combinations. There are many more in the US than in the UK or Europe, many of them obsessed with preppy style. Among the best are 'Ivy League Style' and 'The Trad'. In the UK, the biggest is 'Permanent Style'. But I will pass no comment on its worth, as it is my own.

Although not really a blog and not dedicated to classic style, Scott Schumann's 'The Sartorialist' is a constant inspiration. Nowhere will you find better pictures of Italian classicism and Swedish eccentricity.

Books are much simpler. There aren't many great ones out there, but by far and away the best of dressing well is *Dressing the Man*, by Alan Flusser. And for a history of the suit, with cracking illustrations, go find *Sharp Suits* by Eric Musgrave.

www.styleforum.net
www.askandyaboutclothes.com
www.thelondonlounge.net
www.dresswithstyle.com
www.asuitablewardrobe.dynend.com
www.ivy-style.com
www.thetrad.blogspot.com
www.permanentstyle.co.uk
www.thesartorialist.com

Glossary

6x4 An arrangement of buttons on a double-breasted jacket where, of six buttons on the jacket, only four ever appear to be fastened. The remaining two are show buttons. So 4x4 has four of which all four appear to fasten, etc.

Basting Sewing with loose, long stitches. Usually used to make parts of a jacket easy to disassemble. Hence a basted fitting.

Bird's eye A pattern of small regular circles.

Buggy lining A half lining to a jacket, with nothing on the back of the jacket save one or two sections across the shoulders.

Canvas The inner construction of a suit's chest, usually consisting of a layer of felt and a layer of woven horsehair or wool.

Cashmere The long, fine hair that hircus goats grow through the winter. Combed off by herders in the Spring before it falls off naturally. Very soft and most often used for overcoats and odd jackets.

Chalk stripe A wide stripe on cloth with a little nap, creating a blurred effect.

Pinstripe is thinner and sharper; bead stripe is made up of small dots.

Coat Traditionally, what we now call a jacket: the upper half of a suit. Still called that name by Savile Row tailors. Hence an overcoat goes over the coat. Today, an abbreviation of overcoat.

Collar Section of the jacket directly above the lapel. Different to the lapel in that it is attached separately. The join of the two creates a notch, peak or fish-mouth lapel.

Corduroy Ribbed cotton, originally used as a substitute for velvet. Now used for casual trousers, occasionally odd jackets.

Cuffs Also known as turn-ups, the turned up strip of cloth at the end of a pair of trousers or jacket sleeve.

Flannel Wool without the treatment of worsted, fuzzier with a greater nap.

Flat front Trousers without pleats.

Forepart One half of the front of a jacket, from buttons to side seam. The corresponding part of the back is the backpart.

Fork Where trousers' inside seams meet.

Forward fitting Usually the second fitting for a suit, where all parts are connected but await finishing touches. Easier to change aspects of fit than with a finished suit.

Fresco A patented formulation of worsted wool that is smooth and lightweight.

Gabardine A tight twill in wool, cotton or anything else.

Glenurquhart plaid A check, often referred to as glen plaid, of several closely packed lines. With an overcheck, known as the Prince of Wales after the Duke of Windsor who popularised the pattern.

Gorge The point at which the lapel and collar meet.

Herringbone Essentially a broken twill, creating a zig-zag pattern.

Hopsack A loose weave of worsted wool that is therefore more textured but also breathable.

Horn The traditional material for suit buttons. Made from the horns of animals like cow, deer or buffalo.

Houndstooth Also known as dogtooth, an exploded (enlarged) weave of contrasting colours that creates a jagged pattern.

Midnight blue A very dark blue, almost black.

Mohair Goat hair often used for suitings to be lighter and breathable. Has a slight sheen and therefore sometimes used for evening wear as well.

Nailhead A pattern on cloth of small, regular dots, similar to the tops of nails.

Odd jacket A jacket not worn with matching trousers. Also known as a sports jacket or sports coat.

Pagoda shoulder One where the shoulder line curves slightly upwards.

Paper pattern The plan of a suit that a tailor creates from his measurements. Transferred onto cloth with each new suit, and altered over time as the customer changes.

Pick and pick A weave to cloth that reveals more of the interwoven colours, such as black and white in a grey.

Rise The distance from the fork of a pair of trousers to the waistband.

Roped shoulder One with a raised top to the sleeve.

Scye The armhole of a jacket that the sleeve attaches to.

Seersucker A ribbed cotton cloth popular only in the US.

Skirt The bottom half of a jacket, below the waist.

Strap and buckle Also known as side straps or side tabs, buckles on either side of the trousers' waistband that tighten them.

Suitings, coatings, shirtings Cloth used to make each of those items of clothing.

Super 100s A measurement of the fineness of worsted wool. Originally a measure of how many centimetres the yarn could be stretched to, now codified by the diameter measured in microns.

Tan A pale, caramel-type colour.

Tape A thin strip of material used to close seams when the lack of lining means they are exposed.

Trews Trousers made of one piece of cloth per leg, so neither has a side seam. Often used with checks so they don't have to be matched up at the side.

Tweed Felted or roughly finished wool that is woven with several differently dyed yarns. Not just checked cloth.

Twill A cloth woven into fine cords, usually running diagonally across the cloth.

Waist The slimmest part of your body, between your lungs and hip bones. Around or just above your belly button. As a result, the slimmest point of a jacket and where the waist button is usually positioned. Also often used to refer to the top of trousers, even if worn on the hips.

Windowpane A large check of single lines at least two or three inches apart. When the horizontal and vertical lines are different, a Tattersall check (usually on shirts). Over another check, an overcheck.

Worsted A treated and finely woven wool, what the vast majority of modern suits are made out of.

Index

143

144